THE RAINFOREST

EARTH • AT • RISK

Acid Rain

Alternative Sources of Energy

Animal Welfare

The Automobile and the Environment

Clean Air

Clean Water

Degradation of the Land

Economics and the Environment

Environmental Action Groups

Environmental Disasters

The Environment and the Law

Extinction

The Fragile Earth

Global Warming

The Living Ocean

Nuclear Energy • Nuclear Waste

Overpopulation

The Ozone Layer

The Rainforest

Recycling

Solar Energy

Toxic Materials

What You Can Do for the Environment

Wilderness Preservation

THE RAINFOREST

by Laura Tangley

Introduction by
Russell E. Train

Chairman of
the Board of Directors,
World Wildlife Fund and
the Conservation Foundation

CHELSEA HOUSE PUBLISHERS

new york   philadelphia

CHELSEA HOUSE PUBLISHERS
EDITOR-IN-CHIEF: Remmel Nunn
MANAGING EDITOR: Karyn Gullen Browne
PICTURE EDITOR: Adrian G. Allen
ART DIRECTOR: Maria Epes
ASSISTANT ART DIRECTOR: Howard Brotman
MANUFACTURING DIRECTOR: Gerald Levine
SYSTEMS MANAGER: Lindsey Ottman
PRODUCTION MANAGER: Joseph Romano
PRODUCTION COORDINATOR: Marie Claire Cebrián

EARTH AT RISK
Senior Editor: Jake Goldberg

Staff for *The Rainforest*
ASSOCIATE EDITOR: Karen Hammonds
COPY EDITOR: Ian Wilker
EDITORIAL ASSISTANT: Danielle Janusz
PICTURE RESEARCHER: Villette Harris
SERIES DESIGNER: Maria Epes
SENIOR DESIGNER: Marjorie Zaum
COVER ART: Paul Biniasz
COVER ILLUSTRATION: Janet Hamlin

Library of Congress Cataloging-in Publication Data
Tangley, Laura.
  The rainforest/Laura Tangley; introduction by Russell E. Train.
    p. cm.—(Earth at risk)
  Includes bibliographical references and index.
  Summary: Examines what a rainforest is, its role in maintaining
the Earth's ecosystem, and the causes and consequences of
deforestation.
  ISBN 0-7910-1579-3
       0-7910-1604-8 (pbk.)
  1. Rain forest ecology—Juvenile literature. 2. Rain
forests—Juvenile literature. 3. Deforestation—Tropics—Juvenile
literature. 4. Rain forest conservation—Juvenile literature. [1. Rain
forests. 2. Rain forest ecology. 3. Ecology. 4.
Deforestation—Tropics.] I. Title. II. Series.   91-37270
QH541.5.R27T36 1992   CIP
574.5'2642'0913—dc20   AC

C O N T E N T S

Introduction—Russell E. Train   6

1 The Vanishing Forest   13

2 What Is a Tropical Rainforest?   23

3 The World's Most Diverse Ecosystem   39

4 People and the Rainforest   51

5 Causes of Rainforest Destruction   67

   Picture Essay   71

6 Consequences of Deforestation   91

7 Solutions   105

   Appendix: For More Information   122

   Further Reading   124

   Glossary   126

   Conversion Table   129

   Index   130

INTRODUCTION

Russell E. Train

Administrator, Environmental Protection Agency, 1973 to
1977; Chairman of the Board of Directors, World Wildlife
Fund and The Conservation Foundation

There is a growing realization that human activities increasingly
are threatening the health of the natural systems that make life possible
on this planet. Humankind has the power to alter nature fundamentally,
perhaps irreversibly.

This stark reality was dramatized in January 1989 when *Time*
magazine named Earth the "Planet of the Year." In the same year, the
Exxon *Valdez* disaster sparked public concern over the effects of human
activity on vulnerable ecosystems when a thick blanket of crude oil
coated the shores and wildlife of Prince William Sound in Alaska. And,
no doubt, the 20th anniversary celebration of Earth Day in April 1990
renewed broad public interest in environmental issues still further. It is
no accident then that many people are calling the years between 1990
and 2000 the "Decade of the Environment."

And this is not merely a case of media hype, for the 1990s will
truly be a time when the people of the planet Earth learn the meaning of
the phrase "everything is connected to everything else" in the natural
and man-made systems that sustain our lives. This will be a period when
more people will understand that burning a tree in Amazonia adversely
affects the global atmosphere just as much as the exhaust from the cars
that fill our streets and expressways.

Central to our understanding of environmental issues is the
need to recognize the complexity of the problems we face and the

relationships between environmental and other needs in our society. Global warming provides an instructive example. Controlling emissions of carbon dioxide, the principal greenhouse gas, will involve efforts to reduce the use of fossil fuels to generate electricity. Such a reduction will include energy conservation and the promotion of alternative energy sources, such as nuclear and solar power.

The automobile contributes significantly to the problem. We have the choice of switching to more energy efficient autos and, in the longer run, of choosing alternative automotive power systems and relying more on mass transit. This will require different patterns of land use and development, patterns that are less transportation and energy intensive.

In agriculture, rice paddies and cattle are major sources of greenhouse gases. Recent experiments suggest that universally used nitrogen fertilizers may inhibit the ability of natural soil organisms to take up methane, thus contributing tremendously to the atmospheric loading of that gas—one of the major culprits in the global warming scenario.

As one explores the various parameters of today's pressing environmental challenges, it is possible to identify some areas where we have made some progress. We have taken important steps to control gross pollution over the past two decades. What I find particularly encouraging is the growing environmental consciousness and activism by today's youth. In many communities across the country, young people are working together to take their environmental awareness out of the classroom and apply it to everyday problems. Successful recycling and tree-planting projects have been launched as a result of these budding environmentalists who have committed themselves to a cleaner environment. Citizen action, activated by youthful enthusiasm, was largely responsible for the fast-food industry's switch from rainforest to domestic beef, for pledges from important companies in the tuna industry to use fishing techniques that would not harm dolphins, and for the recent announcement by the McDonald's Corporation to phase out polystyrene "clam shell" hamburger containers.

Despite these successes, much remains to be done if we are to make ours a truly healthy environment. Even a short list of persistent issues includes problems such as acid rain, ground-level ozone and smog, and airborne toxins; groundwater protection and nonpoint sources of pollution, such as runoff from farms and city streets; wetlands protection; hazardous waste dumps; and solid waste disposal, waste minimization, and recycling.

Similarly, there is an unfinished agenda in the natural resources area: effective implementation of newly adopted management plans for national forests; strengthening the wildlife refuge system; national park management, including addressing the growing pressure of development on lands surrounding the parks; implementation of the Endangered Species Act; wildlife trade problems, such as that involving elephant ivory; and ensuring adequate sustained funding for these efforts at all levels of government. All of these issues are before us today; most will continue in one form or another through the year 2000.

Each of these challenges to environmental quality and our health requires a response that recognizes the complex nature of the problem. Narrowly conceived solutions will not achieve lasting results. Often it seems that when we grab hold of one part of the environmental balloon, an unsightly and threatening bulge appears somewhere else.

The higher environmental issues arise on the national agenda, the more important it is that we are armed with the best possible knowledge of the economic costs of undertaking particular environmental programs and the costs associated with not undertaking them. Our society is not blessed with unlimited resources, and tough choices are going to have to be made. These should be informed choices.

All too often, environmental objectives are seen as at cross-purposes with other considerations vital to our society. Thus, environmental protection is often viewed as being in conflict with economic growth, with energy needs, with agricultural productions, and so on. The time has come when environmental considerations must be fully integrated into every nation's priorities.

One area that merits full legislative attention is energy efficiency. The United States is one of the least energy efficient of all the industrialized nations. Japan, for example, uses far less energy per unit of gross national product than the United States does. Of course, a country as large as the United States requires large amounts of energy for transportation. However, there is still a substantial amount of excess energy used, and this excess constitutes waste. More fuel efficient autos and home heating systems would save millions of barrels of oil, or their equivalent, each year. And air pollutants, including greenhouse gases, could be significantly reduced by increased efficiency in industry.

I suspect that the environmental problem that comes closest to home for most of us is the problem of what to do with trash. All over the world, communities are wrestling with the problem of waste disposal. Landfill sites are rapidly filling to capacity. No one wants a trash and garbage dump near home. As William Ruckelshaus, former EPA administrator and now in the waste management business, puts it, "Everyone wants you to pick up the garbage and no one wants you to put it down!"

At the present time, solid waste programs emphasize the regulation of disposal, setting standards for landfills, and so forth. In the decade ahead, we must shift our emphasis from regulating waste disposal to an overall reduction in its volume. We must look at the entire waste stream, including product design and packaging. We must avoid creating waste in the first place. To the greatest extent possible, we should then recycle any waste that is produced. I believe that, while most of us enjoy our comfortable way of life and have no desire to change things, we also know in our hearts that our "disposable society" has allowed us to become pretty soft.

Land use is another domestic issue that might well attract legislative attention by the year 2000. All across the United States, communities are grappling with the problem of growth. All too often, growth imposes high costs on the environment—the pollution of aquifers; the destruction of wetlands; the crowding of shorelines; the loss of wildlife habitat; and the loss of those special places, such as a historic structure or area, that give a community a sense of identity. It is worth noting that growth is not only the product of economic development but of population movement. By the year 2010, for example, experts predict that 75% of all Americans will live within 50 miles of a coast.

It is important to keep in mind that we are all made vulnerable by environmental problems that cross international borders. Of course, the most critical global conservation problems are the destruction of tropical forests and the consequent loss of their biological capital. Some scientists have calculated extinction rates as high as 11 species per hour. All agree that the loss of species has never been greater than at the present time; not even the disappearance of the dinosaurs can compare to today's rate of extinction.

In addition to species extinctions, the loss of tropical forests may represent as much as 20% of the total carbon dioxide loadings to the atmosphere. Clearly, any international approach to the problem of global warming must include major efforts to stop the destruction of forests and to manage those that remain on a renewable basis. Debt for nature swaps, which the World Wildlife Fund has pioneered in Costa Rica, Ecuador, Madagascar, and the Philippines, provide a useful mechanism for promoting such conservation objectives.

Global environmental issues inevitably will become the principal focus in international relations. But the single overriding issue facing the world community today is how to achieve a sustainable balance between growing human populations and the earth's natural systems. If you travel as frequently as I do in the developing countries of Latin America, Africa, and Asia, it is hard to escape the reality that expanding human populations are seriously weakening the earth's resource base. Rampant deforestation, eroding soils, spreading deserts, loss of biological diversity, the destruction of fisheries, and polluted and degraded urban environments threaten to spread environmental impoverishment, particularly in the tropics, where human population growth is greatest.

It is important to recognize that environmental degradation and human poverty are closely linked. Impoverished people desperate for land on which to grow crops or graze cattle are destroying forests and overgrazing even more marginal land. These people become trapped in a vicious downward spiral. They have little choice but to continue to overexploit the weakened resources available to them. Continued abuse of these lands only diminishes their productivity. Throughout the developing world, alarming amounts of land rendered useless by overgrazing and poor agricultural practices have become virtual wastelands, yet human numbers continue to multiply in these areas.

From Bangladesh to Haiti, we are confronted with an increasing number of ecological basket cases. In the Philippines, a traditional focus of U.S. interest, environmental devastation is widespread as deforestation, soil erosion, and the destruction of coral reefs and fisheries combine with the highest population growth rate in Southeast Asia.

Controlling human population growth is the key factor in the environmental equation. World population is expected to at least double to about 11 billion before leveling off. Most of this growth will occur in the poorest nations of the developing world. I would hope that the United States will once again become a strong advocate of international efforts to promote family planning. Bringing human populations into a sustainable balance with their natural resource base must be a vital objective of U.S. foreign policy.

Foreign economic assistance, the program of the Agency for International Development (AID), can become a potentially powerful tool for arresting environmental deterioration in developing countries. People who profess to care about global environmental problems— the loss of biological diversity, the destruction of tropical forests, the greenhouse effect, the impoverishment of the marine environment, and so on—should be strong supporters of foreign aid planning and the principles of sustainable development urged by the World Commission on Environment and Development, the "Brundtland Commission."

If sustainability is to be the underlying element of overseas assistance programs, so too must it be a guiding principle in people's practices at home. Too often we think of sustainable development only in terms of the resources of other countries. We have much that we can and should be doing to promote long-term sustainability in our own resource management. The conflict over our own rainforests, the old growth forests of the Pacific Northwest, illustrates this point.

The decade ahead will be a time of great activity on the environmental front, both globally and domestically. I sincerely believe we will be tested as we have been only in times of war and during the Great Depression. We must set goals for the year 2000 that will challenge both the American people and the world community.

Despite the complexities ahead, I remain an optimist. I am confident that if we collectively commit ourselves to a clean, healthy environment we can surpass the achievements of the 1980s and meet the serious challenges that face us in the coming decades. I hope that today's students will recognize their significant role in and responsibility for bringing about change and will rise to the occasion to improve the quality of our global environment.

THE RAINFOREST

Rainforests provide magnificent scenery as well as vital habitat for more than half the species on earth.

chapter 1

THE VANISHING FOREST

If the destruction is allowed to run its course, Earth will suffer the most devastating blow to life in all our history.
—Thomas E. Lovejoy, Smithsonian Institution

A few years ago, E. O. Wilson, a distinguished Harvard University biologist, identified 43 different species of ants on a single tree in the Peruvian Amazon—about the same number of ant species living in England, Ireland, Scotland, and Wales combined. In an Indonesian rainforest, another Harvard biologist, Peter Ashton, counted 700 tree species in 10 1-hectare (2.5-acre) plots, the same number found on the entire North American continent.

These examples are not isolated cases. Biologists who study birds, beetles, lizards, butterflies, or almost any kind of organism would have a similar story to tell. Tropical rainforests, which grow only in a narrow zone surrounding the equator, are by far the world's most biologically diverse natural habitat. Although they cover less than 7% of the earth's land area, they contain at least half of all plant and animal species. Green, lush, and bursting with life, rainforests are as mysterious as they are

Moderate to severe deforestation is occurring in nations throughout the tropics.

Source: UN Food and Agriculture Organization

beautiful. Up until the present, biologists have identified only a fraction of the forests' millions of species, and they know almost nothing about the lives of most that have been discovered.

Long before these mysteries are solved, however, rain-forests may be gone. Tropical forests of all kinds once covered more than 4 billion acres, an area twice the size of the United States. Already, more than half of these forests have disappeared, and another 51 million acres are lost each year. And when the forests go, the myriad plants and animals that make their home

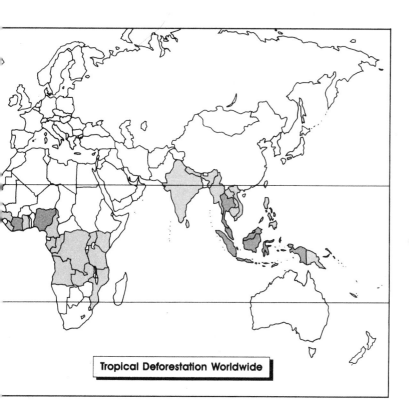

Tropical Deforestation Worldwide

there disappear as well. Some scientists estimate that 1 rainforest species becomes extinct every 15 minutes. If current deforestation rates do not change, they say, most tropical forests and up to a quarter of all the earth's species will be gone forever within the next 25 to 50 years.

The permanent loss of this many of the earth's unique life-forms is in itself a tragedy. But it also may be a threat to human survival. Rainforest plants and animals are the source of many products that have become indispensable to everyday life.

The forests provide food, wood, spices, medicines, oils, fibers, and a wealth of other materials used around the globe. In the United States, one-quarter of all prescription drugs contain active ingredients derived from plants, mostly from the tropics. Because so many species remain undiscovered, the rainforest offers virtually unlimited possibilities for new products in the future. Rainforests also play a key role in regulating water cycles and climate—both locally and globally—so their loss has the potential to upset these vital processes worldwide.

If they are so important, why are tropical rainforests being destroyed? One answer is that rainforests are being lost to commercial logging, agriculture, cattle ranching, and development projects such as dams, roads, and mines. But beneath these immediate causes are several driving forces that leave few other options for the people actually clearing tracts of forest. These forces include overpopulation, poverty, hunger, unfair land distribution, and the huge debts that most developing countries that have rainforests owe to industrialized countries such as the United States.

These issues make tropical deforestation a unique environmental problem. For the most part, the problem cannot be simplified into a case of good versus evil—as is often the scenario when a rich industry pollutes an innocent community's air and water. Deforestation is a far more complicated problem, and it is far more difficult to solve. Thus, what might seem an easy solution to the problem could instead worsen it. Boycotts of tropical products, for example, may cripple a developing country's already-faltering economy so much that it accelerates rather than slows deforestation.

This book will take the reader through this complicated maze of issues by starting at the beginning: What is a tropical rainforest? What kinds of plants, animals, and human societies live in them? In what ways do people around the world depend on rainforests? Why are they being destroyed? What happens after the forests are lost? And, most important, what kinds of actions can stop rainforest destruction?

The forest described in these pages is a composite of a typical lowland rainforest, also known as a moist evergreen forest. The characteristics of an actual rainforest vary according to an area's altitude, rainfall, sunlight, soil composition, and the mixture of plants and animals that have evolved there. In addition to rainforests, there are other kinds of tropical forests, including *deciduous* ones—also called tropical dry forests—in which trees lose their leaves during a dry season just as they do during autumn in the North. The temperate zone even has some rainforests (although they look very different), including the last stands of the ancient, primary forest that once blanketed the U.S. Pacific Northwest.

That these northern primary forests are nearly gone—not only in the United States but also in Canada and most of the remaining temperate zone—illustrates an important point. Today's tropical nations are doing nothing that the industrialized countries have not already done to their own forests. When European colonists arrived in the New World in the 17th century, they began furiously clearing forests for their crops, cattle, roads, and towns. Pushing westward, the settlers cleared more than a third of all U.S. forests by the 1920s.

But colonists on the frontiers of today's tropics are less lucky than those that settled in the North, for reasons that are both biological and sociological. In temperate forests, the nutrients needed for both forest and crop growth lie within these forests' rich, dark soils. But in most tropical rainforests, soils are poor, and nutrients are instead bound up in living vegetation. When forests are cleared, the nutrients in the soil are soon washed away in the rain, causing farms to fail after just a few years and forcing farmers to move on and clear more rainforest. Today's residents of tropical nations also face enormous problems, such as over-

Fifty million acres of tropical forest are destroyed yearly, and scientists fear that much of the remainder will vanish within the next 25 to 50 years.

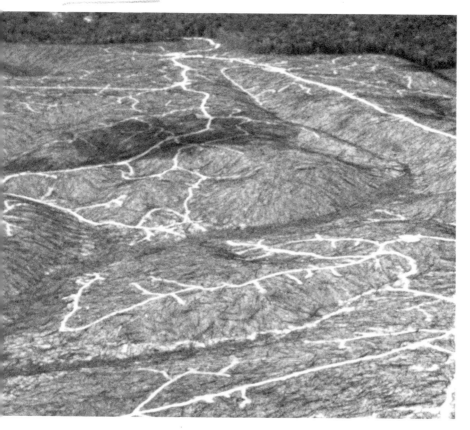

population and crushing poverty, that early settlers in the temperate zone never dreamed of.

This book is written for today's citizens of northern nations. Although most tropical rainforests belong to developing countries, ultimately the demands of the industrialized countries and their control of international trade determine whether the poorer countries can resist exploiting their forests. The book is dedicated particularly to the young people who will govern the rich nations over the next three or four decades. It is within that period of time that the fate of the world's tropical rainforests will be decided.

WHERE HAVE ALL "OUR" BIRDS GONE?

Warblers, tanagers, orioles, and thrushes are among North America's most beautiful and musical signs of spring. But while U.S. and Canadian citizens think of these songbirds as "theirs," the birds actually spend as much, or more, time living in the rainforests of Latin America and the Caribbean. After breeding and raising their chicks in North America during spring and summer, the birds head south to the tropics for the next six to nine months.

Sadly, the populations of many of these songbirds are falling dramatically. Data from the annual North American Breeding Bird Survey show that between 1978 and 1987 the populations of several species declined, including the wood thrush (by 30%), the northern (Baltimore) oriole (by 23%), the scarlet tanager (by 10%), the American redstart (by 10%), and Wilson's warbler (by 45%).

Scientists say these population drops are tied to tropical deforestation. According to tropical biologist John Terborgh of Princeton University, rainforest loss has forced birds that in summer are spread out across more than 6 million square miles to squeeze into less than 1 million square miles in winter. "The unsettling implication," Terborgh writes in *Where Have All the Birds Gone?*, "is that the felling of 1 hectare of rain forest for cattle pasture in Mexico or the Dominican Republic is equivalent in its effect to the construction of a 5- or 10-hectare shopping mall in Connecticut."

Shopping malls, meanwhile, *are* going up in Connecticut—and throughout the birds' summer habitat in the United States and Canada. North Americans therefore are not entirely blameless for the disappearance of their favorite songbirds. Although northern temperate forests still have enough space for the birds, the suburban shops, lawns, gardens, and garbage cans that now surround these forests have provided ideal conditions to attract animals such as jays, crows, raccoons, and opossums that eat songbird eggs and kill hatchlings. These predators take a tremendous toll on migratory songbird populations.

The wood thrush is one of the migrating songbirds losing habitat in both North America and the tropics.

Patches of sunlight illuminate the interior of a rainforest in the Fumée Mountains of French Guiana, South America.

chapter 2

WHAT IS A TROPICAL RAINFOREST?

To understand what is so special about tropical rainforests, it helps to imagine taking a giant step back from the earth and to consider the forests' position on the planet as it revolves around the sun. Straddling the equator between 23°27′ north latitude—known to ancient mariners as the Tropic of Cancer—and 23°27′ south latitude—the Tropic of Capricorn—runs a broad band of the earth's surface known as the Torrid Zone, or tropics. Between these latitudes, the position of the sun is more directly overhead than it is anywhere else in the world. Reaching across 93 million miles of space, the sun's radiant energy strikes the tropics at an almost perpendicular angle, which prevents the atmosphere from scattering many of the rays and ensures that they strike just a small portion of the planet's surface area.

To the north and south of these latitudes, the tilt of the earth's axis of rotation forces the sun's energy to travel through the atmosphere obliquely, at a less than perpendicular angle. When sunlight passes through a longer wedge of atmosphere, more energy is scattered, and when it does reach the ground in these regions, the angle of impact spreads this energy over a wider surface area so that less is absorbed by a given area of land. The tilted spin of the earth in these temperate regions creates the seasons, or times of the year when warmer or cooler temperatures prevail, as the rotating earth leans toward or away from the sun. In winter and summer, the days and nights are of unequal length. But in the tropics, there is neither winter nor summer, spring nor fall. All year, the days and nights are of relatively equal length, and the sun beats down with an intensity that is difficult for people living outside this region to imagine.

Around the equator the resulting warm air expands, becomes less dense, and rises. Cooler, moist air—known as the trade winds—rushes in from both the north and the south and pours into the tropical convergence, a pattern of atmospheric circulation in which heat and moisture accumulate. The inflowing wet air, first heated, then forced upward and cooled, releases its moisture in frequent heavy rainfalls. Other parts of the world— from high northern deserts to eastern U.S. cities—can get hotter than the tropics, but no other areas experience such steady warmth, with high humidities and heavy rains, year-round.

Much of this belt circling the earth's midsection falls over the oceans. But where it lies over land—across much of Central America and northern South America; west central Africa; parts of the Southeast Asian peninsula; the archipelagos, or island chains, of the South Pacific; and parts of New Zealand and northern Australia—the abundance of light, heat, and moisture has created an environment in which living things have flourished and diversified as nowhere else on the planet.

Not all land in the tropics supports rainforests. There are other kinds of tropical forest—including deciduous forests, described in the previous chapter—and nonforest ecosystems such as grasslands, deserts, and high-mountain plains. Rainforests thrive only at low- to midelevations—areas where the temperature never goes below freezing and normally ranges between 75 degrees and 80 degrees Fahrenheit, and at least 60 inches of rain fall each year. Many rainforests receive as much as 100 to 200 inches of rain, and in some very wet forests, such as the northwest coast of Colombia, almost 400 inches fall annually. By contrast, Chicago, Illinois, receives an average of a little more than 30 inches of rainfall a year.

LAYERS OF LIFE

Tropical rainforests are tremendously complex systems. To simplify their study, biologists divide this *ecosystem* into horizontal layers—the forest floor, understory, canopy, and emergent layers—each of which has a different microclimate. These distinctions, however, are somewhat arbitrary, and no parcel of real rainforest will display such clear-cut divisions.

Walking into a tropical rainforest for the first time is an unforgettable experience. It is like nowhere else one has ever been before: The air is perfectly still, the humidity is high, and it takes some time to get used to the semidarkness. Of the abundant sunlight that strikes the roof of a rainforest, only about 2% reaches the forest floor. When it rains, much of the rain, too, is intercepted by the thick vegetation above, which, like a giant sponge, absorbs the water and then releases it slowly and steadily. The dense canopy of trees also protects the forest interior from harsh winds and dryness. The rainforest thus creates its own climate of constant warm, wet conditions, which Charles Darwin called "one great wild, untidy luxuriant hothouse, made by nature for herself."

Many people call rainforests jungles—from the Sanskrit word *jangala*, meaning an impenetrable tangle of trees—but the word is misleading. Vegetation usually is sparse on the forest floor, and one can walk about quite easily. The boles, or trunks, of tropical trees can be enormous, but the trees grow tall and straight like telephone poles, wasting little energy putting out branches until they reach the sunlit canopy 100 or more feet above. Many of the trees are supported by large buttresses or stilt roots extending out from their base. Although some trees outside the tropics—the California redwood, for example—may be taller, the overall visual effect of tropical tree growth is impressive. Growth continues all year round, and unlike trees of the temperate zone, tropical trees exhibit no growth rings along their cross sections. Most of them do not shed their leaves in seasonal cycles, and those that do—usually during the time of year that receives the least rainfall—do so only briefly.

Something that anyone familiar with temperate forests will notice the first time they visit a rainforest is the lack of leaf litter underfoot. In the tropics, litter can decompose in as few as 6

Many rainforest trees have buttressed roots that flare out at the base of the tree, helping support it.

weeks, 60 times faster than in a typical northern evergreen forest. Another striking difference is the thinness of the topsoil and its reddish yellow color. Most tropical rainforests grow on soils called *oxisols*, which are old and nutrient-poor as a result of many years of leaching—the draining away of soil nutrients—by rainfall. Some minerals that resist leaching, specifically aluminum and iron, stay behind in the soil and give it its color. By contrast, soils supporting temperate forests tend to be brown, deep, and rich in nutrients.

It may seem strange that the world's richest forests manage to grow on such poor soils. But rainforest trees have, through evolution, developed special mechanisms that allow them to thrive under what seem to be adverse conditions. All across the forest floor, under the thin layer of leaf litter and running through the topsoil, are threadlike networks of *mycorrhizae*, the feeding structures of fungi that attach themselves to dead leaves, twigs, and bits of insect and animal matter decomposing on the ground. The fungi are attached also to the shallow roots of rainforest trees, so that decaying matter is quickly broken down and digested and the nutrients—most important, potassium and phosphorous—are recycled to the living trees. The whole process is amazingly efficient, but it means that most of the rainforest's nutrients are held within the biomass, or living plants and animals, contained in the forest. The biomass itself, not the land, is the sustainer of this lush ecosystem. Without this complex, painstakingly evolved *system* of forest life, the land itself would be less productive than the land under the wheat fields of Kansas. Sweep away the rainforest, and the soil cannot regenerate it.

Helping recycle nutrients, many creatures scavenge the forest floor. Worms, flies, maggots, and beetles live off the excrement of larger animals. There are millipedes, carnivorous centipedes, scorpions, spiders, and the huge bird-eating tarantula with a leg span of 7 inches. Ground-feeding birds and mammals also abound, digging in the soil for food or grazing on vegetation. These animals include herds of peccary (a type of wild pig) and rodents such as the paca, agouti, and capybara (the world's largest rodent). Also common, but hard to spot on the forest floor, are snakes, including beautifully banded coral snakes and deadly pit vipers such as the bushmaster and fer-de-lance.

Most of these animals scurry out of the way when they hear humans approaching. But there is one group of animals that even the loudest and least-observant forest visitor cannot help but see: the ubiquitous social insects. All over the forest floor, on plants, and up and down the trunks of trees swarm countless varieties of ants and termites. One of the most conspicuous—and fascinating—insect species is the leaf-cutter ant. Out of the corners of their eyes, forest visitors first become aware of a long line of flickering green specks. On closer inspection, it seems as if tiny pieces of leaves have picked themselves up and started marching across the forest floor. But an even closer look reveals that each tiny chunk of leaf is being held upright in the jaw of an ant. The ants have followed a chemical trail laid down by one of their scouts, stretching perhaps hundreds of feet from their underground nest to one of their favorite trees or shrubs. The column runs from the ground right up a trunk or stalk into the foliage. Large ants with strong mandibles, or jaws, travel in both directions, some empty-mouthed and moving toward the tree to begin cutting and slicing foliage, others laden with leaves and headed back to the colony. Other ants—each a member of a caste with a specific job to do—perform different tasks, with the

The capybara, a hefty rodent measuring about 4 feet long and weighing up to 140 pounds, feeds along rivers and lakes in Central and South America.

smallest of all riding on top of leaves held aloft by their nestmates, warding off flies. Back in the nest, the leaves are chewed into a mulch and fed to fungi that in turn provide food for the ants.

It will not surprise anyone who has visited a rainforest to learn that in terms of sheer mass or weight, the ants, termites, and other social insects, such as bees and wasps, compose the greatest amount of living animal material in this environment. Pound for pound, there are more of these insects in the rainforest than there are birds, mammals, amphibians, reptiles, or anything else—except for the plants themselves. By sheer force of their numbers and weight, these tiny animals play a more important role in running the rainforest (and other ecosystems)—pollinating plants and eating and changing the composition of vegetation, for example—than do the far more familiar large mammals. Biologist E. O. Wilson has dubbed insects "the little things that run the world."

RACE TO THE TOP

The next layer above the forest floor is the understory, primarily made up of broad-leaved shrubs, dwarf palms, and immature trees that survive on the few weak shafts of sunlight that penetrate the canopy. These smaller trees are waiting. Should a strong wind or a bolt of lightning bring down one of the forest giants, the small trees will shoot up, and seeds that had been lying dormant in the ground will sprout, each of them racing upward to drink in the precious sunlight that suddenly has flooded this small patch of forest. Within a few years, this gap will be completely filled in with fast-growing saplings. But as more time passes, many of these trees, known as pioneer species, will die, and the more shade-tolerant canopy species will continue their long march upward to reach the canopy.

The determination of which species make it to the top is largely as a result of chance—factors such as the kinds of seeds that were dropped in that spot by a bird, and, of these, which seeds were missed by hungry insect, bird, and mammal foragers. Many rainforest trees rely on disturbances such as tree fall gaps for their survival. Tropical forester Gary Hartshorn found that in Costa Rican rainforests, for example, 75% of the trees need the light gaps created by fallen trees to germinate and grow to maturity. This process also helps maintain the diversity of rainforests.

When an old tree falls, it is unlikely that the same species will grow up to replace it.

Many exotic insects inhabit the understory, including poisonous caterpillars and brilliantly colored grasshoppers, butterflies, and beetles. There are stick insects, whose shape and color make them difficult to distinguish from twigs, and katydids, whose wings have evolved to mimic leaves with remarkable perfection. These creatures are food for animals such as geckos, chameleons, and brightly colored tree frogs, which in turn provide food for such creatures as the vine snake and the eyelash viper.

The understory also teems with the activity of hummingbirds and sunbirds (birds of Africa and Asia that resemble hummingbirds) searching for food. Strong, rapidly beating wings and long beaks enable these tiny birds to hover and sip nectar from the orchids and other flowers clinging to the sides of trees. Small mammals inhabit this layer as well, including coatis, lemurs, loris, anteaters, and tree kangaroos, all with hands and feet specially adapted for clinging to tree limbs. These animals are in turn hunted by the magnificent emerald tree boa or by tree-climbing cats, such as the leopard, ocelot, and jaguar. Although large and beautiful, these cats are hard to find; they are rare,

Climbing vines called lianas wind through the rainforest, forming elaborate, twisting coils as they travel from tree to tree.

A frog-eating bat from Panama. There is a tremendous variety of bats in rainforests, including fruit-eating, bird-eating, lizard-eating, and the infamous vampire—or blood-lapping—species.

extremely wary, and well camouflaged by spots that let them blend perfectly into the dappled sunlit vegetation surrounding them.

Even less rare rainforest animals—including birds—are difficult to see. Many visitors, in fact, are disappointed the first time they walk into the forest. Although they are impressed with the fantastic variety of vegetation growing around them, travelers may see little more than this monotonous wall of green. The rainforest is notoriously slow at giving up its secrets—and it does so only to those who are patient enough to spend some time standing or sitting quietly, looking at and listening to everything around them.

Another reason that visitors see few animals in the rainforest is that most of the action happens way over their heads, 100 to 200 feet above the ground in the forest's canopy layer. Formed by the widely spreading, umbrellalike tops of tall trees, the canopy is characterized by extremes. Its topmost layer is exposed to torrential rains, high winds, and the relentless tropical sun. Poking up through the canopy, although not in a continuous layer, are the real giants of the forest—the emergents—which, without close neighbors, are exposed to even harsher weather conditions. These trees produce leaves that are small and tough, designed to cut down on water loss through evaporation. But a little bit lower, inside the cooler, more shaded canopy, the same tree may grow larger leaves built to intercept light better. Capturing sunlight is the key to success in the canopy, for it is within this layer that the trees convert solar energy, through the process of *photosynthesis,* into the usable energy—food—that drives the entire rainforest ecosystem.

The canopy is home also to the vast majority of rainforest organisms—and, scientists now believe, the majority of life-forms on earth. Within this dense tangle of plants, tree branches, and vines, many creatures live their entire lives, never venturing near the ground. Here, too, are the seeds, fruits, nectars, and leaves that feed thousands of insects and other animals, which in turn feed thousands more species.

In addition to the crowns of the trees themselves, many other kinds of plants make their home in the canopy, relying on the large trees for support. Thick, ropelike woody climbing vines, known as lianas, sprout from the ground and by means of hooked tendrils grow up the sides of the trees, curling and twisting themselves around trunks and limbs until they reach the canopy. There they snake their way through the tree tops and produce their own crowns of leaves, competing for light. Lianas, which grow to lengths of several hundred feet, can grow across as well as up and down several trees, weaving the canopy together with a kind of irregular stitching. Because of their need for support, lianas have evolved a tendency to coil as they grow. Their winding forms are fascinating. If two lianas meet, they may twist around each other several times before pushing upward again, providing a perfect niche in space for a nest of wasps, bees, or ants.

Many of the tall trees are festooned also with epiphytic plants. Unlike true *parasites*, which steal nutrients from their host organisms, *epiphytes* use the trees only for physical support. About 10,000 species of orchids, for example, cling to the trees and draw water from their surfaces. These exquisite flowers attract equally exquisite butterflies and hummingbirds who act as pollinators as they sip the flowers' nectar.

One of the most interesting epiphytic plants is the *bromeliad*, a member of the pineapple family. A bromeliad seed is dropped by a bird into the crook of a tree limb, where it "nests" in a tiny patch of leaf debris and dirt. If the branch lies over a river or floodwaters, the plant may send tenuous roots down from its perch, but for the most part such plants exist independently of the ground. The tank bromeliads open up like flowers with a circular pattern of strong, broad leaves, forming a bowl that collects rainwater. Some of the larger plants may hold several gallons of water. This tiny pond high in the trees forms a miniature ecosystem that is home to bacteria, protozoa, mosquito and dragonfly larvae, worms, snails, salamanders, frogs, and crabs.

There may be as many as 200 different kinds of organisms living within or feeding from a single tank bromeliad.

Other species of bromeliads attach themselves to the tree bark and produce thick, spiny leaves, stiff with water, resembling green porcupines. These epiphytes are prolific and sometimes cover trees—and even fence posts, telephone wires, and rain gutters—completely. It is these and other bromeliads and climbing plants that give a tropical rainforest its characteristic fuzziness and appearance of overabundant growth.

Some of the animals that live in the canopy are the ones people picture when they first think of rainforests: large, colorful toucans and parrots, monkeys, and bizarre creatures such as sloths. The toucan, with its oversized, brilliantly striped bill, is often used as a symbol of the rainforest. Toucans and their biologically similar cousins in Asia and Africa, the hornbills, feed off the fruits of the tallest trees. The variety of rainforest birds stuns the observer who is familiar only with temperate forests. Their names are almost as exotic as their brilliant colors: the scarlet macaw, the rainbow lorikeet, the violaceous trogon, the rufous-tailed jacamar, the resplendent quetzal, the potoo, the russet-backed oropendola, and the bird of paradise. Many species of bats, both animal- and plant-eating, share the food of the canopy with these birds, feeding at night rather than during the day.

The canopy is home also to many small mammals. The best known, monkeys, are masters of *arboreal*, or treetop, life. Throughout the world's rainforests, monkeys—including gibbons, orangutans, howling monkeys, capuchins, woolly monkeys, and spider monkeys—move through the branches on rainforest trees, alone or in troops, eating fruits, nuts, insects, and leaves. Monkeys of the Old World forests in Africa and Asia are tailless, but monkeys of the New World tropics, or *neotropics,* have prehensile tails that can be manipulated with the dexterity of a fifth limb. With or without tails, monkeys have long, powerful arms and well-developed hands, and they move through the branches with an arm-over-arm motion called brachiation, sometimes with surprising speed.

If monkeys are the fastest-moving canopy mammals, there is no doubt which species is the slowest: the appropriately named sloth. Found only in the neotropics, the sloth has adapted completely to living in the trees and, in fact, can no longer walk upright on the ground. It hangs upside down from long, hooked claws, feeding—very slowly, of course—on fruits and leaves, digesting this food at a sloth's pace as well. But their slowness does not mean sloths are caught by predators more often than are speedier animals. Sloths move so imperceptibly that they are often overlooked, and thick algae growing in their fur help conceal them in the green vegetation.

THE LAST FRONTIER

Until recently, virtually nothing was known about sloths and other rainforest animals that rarely, if ever, come to the

An observation tower constructed in the Amazon aids scientists in studying life in the rainforest canopy.

ground. But the last decade or so has seen revolutionary advances in techniques of studying the forest canopy. Today biologists are exploring the canopy using several ingenious devices, including huge towers and construction cranes, canopy walkways, hot-air balloons, and gear used by mountain climbers to scale rock walls. Through observation and experiments conducted high in the canopy, these scientists have learned a great deal about the plants and animals they once caught only glimpses of through binoculars. Among the most interesting of their discoveries have been thousands of new species of insects—so many, in fact, that the researchers are revising the number of species of organisms they believe inhabit the earth.

So far, biologists have found and named a total of about 1.4 million species of plants and animals. They once believed that there would turn out to be between 1.5 million and 5 million species of living creatures on the planet. But in the early 1980s, that belief was shattered. Pioneering another new technique to explore the rainforest canopy—fogging the treetops with a weak organic pesticide that causes insects to fall into collecting funnels below—Smithsonian Institution entomologist Terry Erwin found so many previously undiscovered beetles living in Peru that he suggested there may be as many as 5 million to 30 million different species on earth, the majority of them insects, and the majority of them living *only* in rainforests.

The hooked beak of the parrot helps it obtain food and crack open nuts and seeds. Over time, species evolve such unique characteristics, or adaptations, which help them survive in a competitive environment.

chapter 3

THE WORLD'S MOST DIVERSE ECOSYSTEM

The biological diversity of rainforests is staggering and, by now, legendary. For instance, although an entire temperate forest may be home to no more than 3 or 4 species of trees—such as oaks, maples, birches, and pines—researchers have found more than 100 kinds of trees in a single acre of tropical forest. In one section of Amazonia only 4 miles square, they have identified 750 different tree species.

The diversity of animals is equally impressive. Colombia, for example, has more than 1,500 species of birds; in the United States, a much larger country, there are only 700 species of native birds. The Amazon Basin, which is one-third the size of the United States and Canada combined, has four times as many species of fish. In one square mile of Peruvian rainforest live more than 1,500 butterfly species, more than in all of North America. And in Panama, researchers have found 12 different insect and mite species living in the fur of a single sloth.

Why have so many species of plants and animals evolved in tropical rainforests? Many experts say the answer lies in the long-term stability of these ecosystems. Rainforests are ancient

habitats, and many of them survived the ice ages that dramatically changed the climate in other parts of the world. Although
other scientists offer different theories of how rainforest diversity
arose—and recent evidence suggests that some forests have been
less stable than was once believed—there is no doubt about what
maintains diversity in these ecosystems: the year-round heat and
rainfall that create constant ideal growing conditions and, just as
important, the adaptations that each species has evolved to
exploit its tiny corner of this great greenhouse.

AN EVOLUTIONARY SHOWCASE

These specially adapted life-forms, ranging from plants
that eat insects to bats that eat frogs, fish that eat fruit, and trees
that strangle other trees, point to one of the principal reasons that
rainforests have excited so much scientific interest. The forests
offer far more than lists of species or entertaining stories about
bizarre creatures. They are living laboratories of biological principles, showcases in which biologists can study life as a dynamic
process, to learn how and why life takes the forms and patterns
that it does. The rainforest is a place where nature readily shows
its logic as well as its beauty.

As Charles Darwin pointed out in 1859 in his classic
book *The Origin of Species,* the great driving engine of all living
systems is the mechanism of *natural selection.* Over time, living
things randomly produce slight variations in their own characteristics of appearance, physiology, and behavior. If these slightly
different organisms are less well equipped to survive, which they
usually are, they will die out. But if these different individuals are
better able to survive and produce more offspring—for example, a

plant whose bigger-than-average leaves capture more sunlight or have chemicals that repel pests—they become the norm. Over eons and millions of random variations, the environment in effect selects and fine-tunes species so that they seem specifically designed for their habitat. This process of adaptation is known as *evolution.*

Evolution is one of biology's most powerful ideas. It explains why the hummingbird's tongue is long enough to sip the nectar from an orchid, why the jaguar's dappled yellow-and-black coat makes it virtually invisible within the mosaic of foliage, and why the hooked beak of a parrot is so efficient at cracking open nuts. Behind every seemingly strange shape and bizarre behavior, there lies the principle of adaptation.

With at least half the world's species living in tropical rainforests, the number of unique adaptations these organisms have evolved and the number of them that involve interactions among different species are enormous. For this reason, rainforests are considered places where strategies for survival have reached their evolutionary pinnacle. As many and diverse as the purposes for these adaptations are, they can be grouped into three broad categories: strategies to get food, to avoid being eaten, and to reproduce.

TO EAT WITHOUT BEING EATEN

There seem to be as many things to eat in a rainforest as there are hungry mouths looking for a meal. And from leaf-cutter ants that farm underground fungus gardens to toucans, whose razor-sharp bills are both agile enough to pluck tiny seeds and strong enough to open them, rainforest animals have evolved sides of other trees or starting their lives high up in the sunlit canopy.

The strangler fig combines the survival strategies of epiphytes and climbers. Its seed begins to grow high in a tree limb like a bromeliad's seed does. It then sends out intertwining ropelike shoots, some growing around and down the host tree to form roots and others growing around and up the tree to produce a crown of leaves. Gradually these runners thicken and form a tightening network of minitrunks that crisscross and completely encase the host tree, while the strangler's crown spreads and overshadows the host tree's leaves. Starved for light from above and deprived of water and nutrients from below, the supporting tree eventually dies and decomposes, leaving the mature fig tree in its place.

To avoid being eaten by the forest's many plant-eating animals, or *herbivores*, plants sport spines, thorns, and stinging hairs, and some have toxic chemicals within their leaves. These toxins, called secondary compounds because they are not substances used directly in the plant's daily metabolism, are the chemicals from which researchers have synthesized drugs used

The aptly named strangler fig germinates in the crown of a tree and sends runners down its trunk, encasing and frequently smothering the host tree.

nearly as many ways to feed on this bounty. Animals that eat food that no other animals want, or that obtain food in unusual ways, are definitely at an advantage. There are species of Amazonian fish, for example, that wait in rivers or flooded forests beneath the boughs of trees to feed on fruits that drop off into the water. One fish even shoots saliva up into the trees to knock down the fruit. Chameleons snare insect meals in a fraction of a second using sticky-tipped tongues that are longer than the reptiles' bodies. And there are many different kinds of birds that hunt together, in groups called mixed-species flocks, each seeking its own particular food but at the same time benefiting the others by stirring up other prey and providing extra pairs of eyes to watch for predators.

For plants, light is the equivalent of food, and rainforest species have adopted many different strategies for obtaining that precious resource. Pioneer trees grow quickly in tree fall gaps, live a short while, then die. Slower-growing canopy trees outlast the pioneers, spreading out horizontally once they reach the light above. Lianas and epiphytes take shortcuts—saving energy that otherwise would be used to construct trunks—by climbing up the

Many bromeliad species take root high up on trees, where they receive more sunlight and water than do plants growing on the dark forest floor.

in modern medicine. Effective as these compounds are, some herbivores have evolved tolerance to the poisons, which also require considerable energy to produce. So plants employ other defensive strategies as well. The passion flower, for example, covers its leaves with tiny bumps that look like the eggs of a butterfly whose caterpillars are cannibalistic—a sure turnoff to another butterfly looking for a place to lay its eggs.

Perhaps the most fascinating defense tactic of plants involves cooperation between plants and ants. One of the classic examples of this strategy involves cecropia trees, common pioneer species of the neotropics. Because they specialize in rapid growth, cecropia trees concentrate on capturing light. They produce large, horizontally spreading leaves and so have little energy left for chemical defense. Instead, some cecropia trees are effectively protected by colonies of Aztec ants that live inside hollow chambers in the trees' trunks. The ants groom their host tree and ferociously defend it from herbivores by biting and secreting irritating chemicals into the bite. In return, the cecropia tree provides a home for the ants and produces tiny energy-rich food parcels, a diet that the ants supplement by raising mealy bugs.

Rainforest animals trying to avoid meat-eating *predators* employ basically the same strategies that temperate-zone species use, but they seem to have refined these tricks to perfection. Camouflage is a good example. The rainforest is filled with animals, insects in particular, that look like something other than what they are: leaf-mimicking katydids that have evolved realistic-looking holes and disease spots, insects that appear to be sticks, and a Malaysian praying mantis that looks exactly like the bright pink orchid on which it perches. Some insects try to look scary. Many moths sport huge, fierce-looking false eyes on their wings, and the

Great Mormon caterpillar looks remarkably similar to the head of a snake.

Like plants, some animals use chemical defenses, and these species tend to advertise their toxicity with bright colors. The poison dart frog, for instance—whose skin is so toxic that Indians use it to coat arrow tips before hunting—is bright red with equally brilliant blue legs. Some animals that are not poisonous imitate deadly species, a phenomenon called *Batesian mimicry*, after the 19th-century-naturalist Henry Walter Bates. The best-known example of mimicry in the temperate zone is the Viceroy butterfly, a perfectly palatable insect that passes for the poisonous Monarch butterfly.

THE BIRDS AND THE BEES

Brightly colored rainforest birds, on the other hand, do not use their hues to advertise that they are poisonous. Instead, they are using a tried-and-true strategy for attracting mates. Brilliant red, yellow, blue, and green males, often adorned by fancy crests and tails, woo drab-colored females, competing for the chance to mate and pass on their genes. Some birds, such as the neotropical manakins and the fantastically decorated birds of

One of the best-camouflaged insects in the rainforest is the walkingstick, here (on the right) almost indistinguishable from its supporting twig (on the left).

paradise of Australia and New Guinea, also perform strange dances and acrobatics to attract females. The male bower bird, which also lives in Australia and New Guinea, constructs an elaborate arbor, the quality of which, biologists believe, determines whether a female will mate with him.

Once successfully mated, animals must do what they can to ensure the survival of their offspring. Again, the strategies used to accomplish this task are diverse. Male Southeast Asian hornbills, for example, hole up both the female and the young inside a tree cavity until the hatchlings are ready to start flying. The female poison dart frog carries its tiny tadpoles 100 feet or more up into the forest canopy, places them in a bromeliad—where they will be safe from aquatic predators below—and then returns once a day to feed her young with one of her own unfertilized eggs.

Plants, too, must reproduce, and because they cannot move—and therefore cannot look for mates—they face particularly difficult challenges. No wonder that the strategies plants have evolved to attract *pollinators*—animals that carry fertilizing pollen from one plant to another—are some of the most complex and interesting of all interactions in the rainforest. The key to pollination success in the forest, where plant species are often rare and widely separated from others of their kind, is specificity. Different plants have evolved flowers of different shapes, colors, and aromas that are designed to attract one, and only one, type of pollinator. There are hummingbird flowers, butterfly flowers, and even bat flowers (which open at night, lack color, and emit a musty, rather than sweet, odor).

Perhaps the strangest strategy a plant has evolved to attract a particular pollinator—or at least the strangest discovered so far—is employed by *Rafflesia arnoldi*, a Southeast Asian plant whose flowers are the world's largest, measuring up to three feet across. To lure the carrion flies it uses to transport pollen, *Rafflesia's* huge blossoms look and smell remarkably like rotting meat, an attraction the flies seem unable to resist. Fig trees, however, may have evolved the most foolproof pollination system of all: These trees are pollinated by tiny wasps that lay their eggs inside the fig's fruits. Worldwide there are 900 species of fig and 900 species of fig wasp, each of which lays its eggs in and pollinates only its own host species.

Once it has been pollinated, a plant has won only half the reproduction battle. It must now get its seeds somewhere where they can germinate (right beneath the tree is both too dark and lacking in nutrients). Unlike most temperate forest trees, whose seeds usually are dispersed by wind, trees of the tropical rainforest rely on animals for seed dispersal. To attract their bird, mammal, or, occasionally, insect seed dispersers, trees produce nutritious, fleshy fruits. After the animals eat the fruit, they deposit the hard, indigestible seeds inside that fruit somewhere away from the parent tree. Like pollination schemes, some seed dispersal strategies are clever—and complex. There is a Costa Rican rainforest tree, for example, that researchers believe uses both birds and ants to get the job done: the birds eat the fruit and defecate the seeds in a random location, and the ants, lured by small, edible substances attached to these seeds, take them to an ideal germination site—their nest's nutrient-rich garbage dump.

A DELICATE BALANCE

From a quick review of these examples, it is clear that most rainforest plants and animals depend heavily on each other, not only to eat, but also to protect themselves and to leave behind a new generation of offspring. This interdependence of creatures—far greater than in temperate forests—makes rainforest ecosystems highly vulnerable to disturbance. For example, if hunters kill off all members of a bird species that pollinates a tree—or all the mammals that disperse its seeds—the tree species will also die out, as will insects and other animals that depend on it. Thus, in the rainforest, losing just one species can set off a chain reaction that affects dozens of others.

The organism whose loss sets off this chain reaction may seem insignificant. The army ant, a familiar feature of many tropical rainforests, is a good example. Raiding columns of these ants—colonies of which may contain a million individuals—hunt the forest floor at night, consuming large numbers of insects and even small frogs and birds.

Although army ants may appear to be useless or even downright malevolent creatures—they will ferociously bite the foot of anyone who blunders into their columns—there are many animals that depend on the ant raids for their survival. As the ants race across the forest floor in columns that can measure up to 100 feet across, they send terrorized insects jumping and flying in all directions. Other insects and birds benefit from the misfortune of the escapees. There are flies, for example, that hover near ant raids, waiting for a fleeing grasshopper, scorpion, or katydid. The fly lays an egg on the larger insect, and when the larva, or offspring, hatches, it burrows into the insect's body and eats it. Many birds, including woodcreepers, cuckoos, motmots, and antbirds, actually follow ant raids, feeding on escaping insects. In one Mexican rainforest, researchers have found that 41 bird species rely on army ant raids for food.

But this complex chain of interdependencies does not end even here: Following the birds that follow the ants are several species of brightly colored butterflies that obtain life-sustaining nitrogen from the birds' droppings. Because rainforests remain somewhat mysterious ecosystems, with countless new species yet to be discovered, biologists may still have just scratched the surface when it comes to finding out which creatures rely on army ants—and on the flies, birds, and butterflies that rely on them. Yet despite their significant role in the tropical forest ecosystem, army ants are vulnerable creatures. In the Amazon, researchers have found that a single colony requires 75 acres of unbroken forest. As rainforests are hacked into smaller and smaller pieces, they may be losing the complex web of life built upon the tiny backs of army ants, and eventually—if the ant or another key species disappears—the entire system, like a perfectly balanced house of cards, could collapse.

Plants have evolved many different strategies for attracting pollinators, including blooming at night, the tactic of this Peruvian cactus flower.

A Yagua Indian in Peru prepares a blowgun dart, used to hunt birds and mammals in the forest. The traditional hunting-and-gathering ways of life of indigenous rainforest peoples are jeopardized by the ongoing destruction of these forests.

chapter 4

PEOPLE AND THE RAINFOREST

As fascinating and important as rainforests are, they can seem remote to people living in industrialized nations. Despite their physical distance, rainforests are in many ways close to home. To see how, one needs only to take a look inside the average home. From the food on the kitchen table to the living-room furniture, clothes in the bedroom, and medicines and cosmetics in the bathroom cabinet, products derived from the rainforest play an important role in everyday life throughout the world.

Most of the staple crops on which people depend for survival came originally from tropical nations. Rice, for example, came from Southeast Asia, corn from Mexico, and potatoes from Peru. Today plant breeders use wild relatives of these crops, also found in the tropics, to develop new, more productive varieties that can resist crop plants' ever-broadening array of insect pests and diseases.

Germ plasm, or genes, taken from the wild relatives of crop plants have come to the rescue of those crops time and time again. In 1970, for example, southern corn leaf blight, a disease caused by a fungus, infected corn plants throughout the midwestern United States causing the loss of 15% of the nation's corn crop, worth $2 billion. To stop further spread of the blight, researchers crossed commercial corn with a related plant, which came originally from Mexico, that was immune to the blight and passed on that resistance to commercial corn.

In addition to staple crops, many of the fruits, nuts, spices, and other foods that make the world's diet more interesting and nutritious came originally from tropical forests. Coffee, for instance, is derived from an Ethiopian forest bush, cocoa from an Amazonian rainforest tree, and sugar from plants growing in Asian forests. Bananas, oranges, mangoes, and papayas came from tropical forests, as did nutmeg, cinnamon, black pepper, and cloves. Some experts say that a full 80% of the world's diet has its origins in the tropics.

When most people think of rainforests, they think of wood rather than food, and indeed these forests provide the world with about a fifth of all wood used in industry. In recent years, global demand for tropical hardwoods has increased dramatically. Prized for their strength and beautiful colors, these woods also are resistant to termites, fungi, and other causes of decay. It would be difficult to find a home in the industrial world today that does not contain any furniture, plywood, wood siding, cutting boards, salad bowls, or other products that were once part of a rainforest tree.

Two of the best known tropical hardwoods are mahogany and teak. The great African mahogany, also known as *khaya*, grows to heights of 200 feet. A light, strong wood with an attractive reddish brown color, it is used in high-quality furniture, boat frames, and *veneers*, thin layers of decorative wood that often cover tables, desks, and hi-fi cabinets. Because this wood is in such high demand, it is becoming rare and expensive, and other mahogany-like tropical woods—utile, sapele, guarea, and crabwood—are harvested as substitutes. Central American mahogany is considered superior to African, but it is even rarer and more expensive. Teak, a highly prized wood valued for its strength and durability, comes from Southeast Asian countries, including India, Burma, Thailand, and Indonesia. Teak's uses include shipbuilding—especially decking—and, because of its resistance to acids, the wood is often found on laboratory benchtops.

Two other tropical woods valued for their aesthetic qualities are rosewood and ebony. Rosewood, which has a dark, purple-brown color, grows in many tropical countries around the world and is used for furniture, cutlery handles, and xylophone keys. A related tree, African blackwood, is fashioned into wind instruments such as clarinets, flutes, and bagpipes. Ebony, also found in many tropical countries, is dark brown or black and is used in furniture, decorative carvings, billiard cues, and musical instruments—particularly the black keys of pianos.

The largest single consumer of tropical hardwoods in the world is Japan, followed closely by the United States. Japan buys nearly a third of all tropical hardwoods on the international market—more than Belgium, Denmark, France, Germany, Greece, Ireland, Italy, Luxembourg, the Netherlands, Portugal, Spain, and the United Kingdom combined. In the United States, demand for hardwoods has been growing at a faster rate than the country's population. Between 1950 and 1973, U.S. tropical hardwood imports increased ninefold, and they are expected to double again by the year 2000. Although these imports meet only

2% of the nation's total wood demand, they represent a large share of tropical hardwood exports. The United States buys about 70% of all tropical veneer and plywood that enters the world market, for example.

MINOR FOREST PRODUCTS

In addition to wood and food, an astonishing array of other everyday products comes from tropical rainforests. Industrialized and developing countries alike use tropical fibers and canes, for instance, to make baskets and wicker furniture, stuff life buoys, and manufacture insulation and soundproofing materials. Essential oils derived from tropical plants make their way into mouthwash, deodorant, cough drops, and other medicine cabinet basics. Edible oils, such as coconut oil and palm oil, are used not only in margarine, mayonnaise, and ice cream but also in such products as detergents, lubricants, cellophane, and candles. Other raw materials derived from tropical forests—including gums, resins (thick fluids that are found in a tree's food-transporting tissues), waxes, tannins, and dyes—turn up in hundreds of products on drugstore, hardware store, and supermarket shelves. Often inappropriately called minor forest products, these important raw materials provide developing nations with a significant amount of revenue.

One of the most valuable nonwood forest products is rubber. Originally derived from the Brazilian *Hevea brasiliensis* tree, rubber grown in Southeast Asia fetches more than $3 billion a year. Natural rubber, in fact, is the fourth largest agricultural export from the developing world. Such indispensable products as tires for automobiles, trucks, aircraft, and the space shuttle cannot be made with synthetic rubber because it is not as elastic and heat resistant as natural rubber. This natural resource is processed for use in such diverse products as adhesives, surgical gloves, balloons, and sneakers. Other rainforest products find their way into clothing as well; crepe-soled shoes and cotton-ramie sweaters, for example, are made from raw materials derived from tropical forests.

Perhaps the most valuable of all rainforest products are the many pharmaceuticals that have been synthesized from forest plants. It is estimated that a fourth of all prescription drugs dispensed in U.S. pharmacies—drugs that are worth approximately $14 billion a year—contain active compounds derived from plants. Most of these chemicals are secondary compounds that the plants have produced to avoid being eaten. Because there are so many species of plants—and plant predators—in tropical forests, the majority of plant compounds scientists have used to

A milky liquid called latex drips from a freshly cut rubber tree into a collecting cup. When the latex hardens, it is processed into rubber and used in products ranging from tires to surgical gloves.

synthesize drugs have come from these forests. Of 3,000 plants the National Cancer Institute has identified as having anticancer properties, for example, 70% live in the rainforest.

One tropical plant, the rosy periwinkle, has already profoundly affected the lives of thousands of people suffering from Hodgkin's disease and childhood leukemia. Drugs derived from compounds in this plant now offer victims of the most common form of childhood leukemia a 75% to 80% chance of recovery and Hodgkin's disease sufferers a 58% chance of recovery. (In 1960, childhood leukemia victims faced a one in five chance of remission, and Hodgkin's disease was nearly always fatal.) Other important drugs that have been derived from tropical plants include tubocurarine, made from the South American vine *Chondrodendron tomentosum* and used as a muscle relaxant during surgery; ouabain, a heart medicine derived from the West African vine *Strophanthus gratus*; and quinine, an antimalaria drug made by boiling the bark of the South American cinchona tree.

The possibility of developing more drugs and other products from rainforests is enormous. So far, scientists have only scratched the surface of the forests' potential for providing chemical compounds that may be useful, or even essential, to human survival. For example, all the plant-derived drugs used in the world today have come from fewer than 90 of the earth's estimated 250,000 plant species. And just 20 plant species provide 90% of the world's food, although thousands of other plants are thought to be edible.

Recent developments in biotechnology, including re-combinant DNA—which allows researchers to move genes from one organism or species to another—have even further increased possibilities for new products from the rainforest. Whereas it can take plant breeders a decade or more to develop a commercially valuable new crop, for example, recombinant DNA technology enables researchers to skip years of breeding experiments in which they aim to develop plants with useful traits but without harmful ones. Recombinant DNA allows them to precisely insert desirable genes from one plant into another without getting unwanted genes in the bargain. But despite its enormous potential, however, recombinant DNA cannot create new genes. All the raw materials that researchers need to develop new foods, drugs, and other products will have to come from living plants and animals, the majority of which live in the tropics.

CULTURAL DIVERSITY

As much as inhabitants of industrialized nations need rainforests, the people who live in these forests depend on them even more directly. Throughout the rainforests of Latin America, Asia, and Africa live hundreds of thousands of such *indigenous*, or native, people. Each indigenous group has its own distinctive language and culture. On the island of New Guinea, for example, live peoples who speak more than 700 different languages. These rainforest inhabitants stand to lose the most from tropical deforestation: not only their homes and livelihoods but also their traditions and ways of life.

With these traditions will go a gold mine of information about rainforests that indigenous peoples have accumulated— and passed on by word of mouth—over thousands of years. This knowledge has benefited people throughout the world. Many of the drugs that scientists have synthesized from compounds in

Indigenous forest peoples traditionally cultivate small plots of land that are far less damaging to fragile rainforest soils than are the large farms established by new-comers.

rainforest plants were developed only because researchers observed the indigenous people who already were using those plants to treat disease. South American Indians, for example, used the bark of the cinchona tree to treat malaria long before researchers began making quinine from it. Indigenous groups also have given the world ideas for new foods. Long a staple in the diet of Southeast Asian forest groups, the protein-rich winged bean, for example, is now improving nutrition in more than 50 nations.

Most indigenous groups of the rainforest support themselves by hunting and gathering. With bows and arrows or blowpipes, hunters capture birds, monkeys, and other small mammals to supplement a diet of fruits and nuts gathered from rainforest plants. Some indigenous groups also clear small patches of forest to grow crops. Passed down through many generations, their farming methods are well suited to the rainforest's fragile soil. Thus, unlike the majority of farms established by recent forest settlers, the farming systems of indigenous groups are sustainable—that is, they continue producing food indefinitely without destroying the forest ecosystem on which they depend.

Whereas the farms of most rainforest immigrants fail after 1 or 2 years, those established by the Amazon's native Kayapó, for example, continue producing food for up to 25 years. One of the Kayapó's secrets is keeping each forest plot small. Another is making use of a diversity of the forest's riches—hunting, fishing, and gathering wild plants—being careful not to overexploit any single source. In all, the Kayapó use about 600 different plant species, eating some and using others for medicines, building materials, oils, paints, dyes, soaps, and even insect repellents.

Until the 1960s, the Lacandon Maya Indians of Mexico's Chiapas rainforests were isolated from the outside world and able to live the same way they had for generations. Although logging roads built in 1965 have brought in hundreds of thousands of colonists and cattle ranchers, the Lacandon Maya who remain—about 450 people—still follow the ancient practices that have allowed them to farm the forest for centuries without destroying it. Respected worldwide for their ecological soundness, Lacandon agricultural systems combine tree crops with food and other crops, an approach known as *agroforestry*. A single plot may produce up to 80 kinds of food and fiber products at the same time. Just as impressively, each plot continues to produce these products for seven years in a row—compared to one or two years for nearby immigrant farms—and even after seven years, rubber, cacao (the source of chocolate), citrus, and other tree crops can be planted successfully. Eventually, the Lacandon allow these plots to return to forest and recover for several years before beginning the cycle over again.

Throughout Africa and Asia, indigenous groups are equally successful at making a living off the forest without destroying it. In Zaire, for example, the Efe pygmies of the Ituri Forest use a variety of plants, gathering more than 100 different species to eat and to make medicines, baskets, dyes, tools, and other essentials. For part of the year, the Efe subsist exclusively on the plants and animals of the forest, spending the remaining months working in the fields of a nearby agricultural group, the Lese, in exchange for food and other goods. In Thailand, about 12,000 Lua people still follow ecologically sound farming practices that have been passed down from their ancestors.

Jute fibers, used to make sacking, burlap, and twine, hang to dry outside a native dwelling in Peru.

The Lua supplement the rice, corn, and sorghum staples they grow with more than 200 wild plant species used for food and other purposes.

If adopted widely, the farming practices of the Lua, Efe, Lacandon Maya, Kayapó, and other rainforest groups could improve the lives of thousands of nonindigenous forest people, most of whom are now barely able to scrape out a living. indigenous knowledge about how to farm fragile rainforest soils sustainably also could reduce the amount of forest destruction. Yet ironically, deforestation is destroying many of these indigenous cultures before they have a chance to pass on this critical knowledge.

GLOBAL LINKS

Perhaps the greatest value of rainforests—to people living in both tropical and temperate regions—is the role the forests play in creating and maintaining the environmental conditions that make human life possible. In this case, the whole ecosystem is indeed greater than the sum of its parts.

Rainforests play a vital role in hydrologic, or water, cycles, for example. Although rainfall in the tropics is abundant, it tends to fall erratically. The typical pattern is several months of heavy rains followed by several dry months in which no rain at all may fall. When the rains return, they are often torrential. Rainforests temper the impact of both heavy downpours and long dry spells by intercepting raindrops before they reach the ground and then releasing the water gradually as it drips from one leaf to another through the forest's successive layers. When the rain finally reaches the ground, it lands slowly and gently enough for the soil to absorb it. The soil, in turn, releases water gradually to rivers and streams. By ensuring this steady flow of water year-round, the rainforest helps prevent both droughts and floods.

One way to visualize the rainforest's role in controlling water flow is to imagine a sponge that soaks up a forceful stream of water from a faucet and is then very, very slowly squeezed dry. Indeed, rainforest expert Norman Myers calls the forest's water-regulating phenomenon the "sponge effect." As long as tropical soils are covered by forests, Myers writes in *The Primary Source*, "rivers not only run clear and clean, they flow throughout the year. When the forest is cleared, rivers start to turn muddy, then swollen or shrunken."

Without their protective forest cover, tropical soils are, depending on the season, exposed to either extreme dryness or rains that fall so hard the soil cannot absorb them. The result is a disastrous cycle of drought followed by flooding. As floodwaters rush down deforested hillsides, they also carry away a tremendous amount of sediment. This soil erosion not only degrades the land so badly that it cannot support new forests or crops, it also damages rivers and streams when sediments wash into these waters. Some sediments make it as far as the ocean, where they are damaging coral reefs and fishing grounds throughout the tropics.

Scientists have discovered recently that rainforests, in addition to controlling the impact of rainfall, often are responsible for *producing* rainfall. For example, in the Brazilian Amazon (one of the wettest regions on earth) about three-fourths of all rain that falls comes directly from water that has either evaporated from leaf surfaces or been released from small openings in leaves

By evaporating rainwater and replenishing clouds overhead, rainforest trees and plants play a crucial role in maintaining the moist climate they need in order to survive.

through the process of transpiration. By replenishing clouds with evaporated water, the Amazon's trees and other plants produce the lion's share of the region's rainfall. Only a quarter of the water ever leaves the system through rivers or streams.

Scientists have also learned that deforestation disrupts this vital system. According to Brazilian researchers, deforestation so dramatically decreases the amount of water evaporated from trees, while simultaneously increasing the amount of water lost through runoff, that it reverses the normal 3:1 rain retention to loss ratio. In other words, three-quarters of all rainfall flows out of the ecosystem, and only one-quarter stays in it. The result is an overall decrease in rainfall that affects all of the remaining forest.

THE GREENHOUSE EFFECT

Tropical rainforests also play a role in regulating the global climate. Their huge trees are major storehouses of carbon, a key element found in all living things as well as in the earth's atmosphere. According to Myers, tropical forests contain about 340 billion tons of carbon, equal to approximately half the carbon in the atmosphere. When forests are cleared—and their trees are burned and replaced by crops, cattle pastures, or towns—this stored carbon is released in the form of the gas carbon dioxide. Scientists estimate that deforestation is adding about 3.1 billion tons of carbon to the atmosphere every year.

This loading of the atmosphere with excess carbon dioxide is cause for concern. Gases such as carbon dioxide play a critical role in maintaining the earth's temperature. When sunlight strikes the planet's surface, some of it is radiated back to space in the form of infrared energy. But carbon dioxide and certain other atmospheric gases (including water vapor, methane, nitrous oxide, ozone, and chlorofluorocarbons) slow the escape of this infrared energy, thereby warming the atmosphere and the surface of the planet. A natural phenomenon, this so-called *greenhouse effect* is what keeps the earth's temperature within a range suitable for living things. In contrast, Mars, which has a thin atmosphere low in these gases, has a surface temperature of -76° Fahrenheit, whereas equally lifeless Venus, with a dense blanket of greenhouse gases, has a surface temperature so hot it can melt lead.

As necessary to life as carbon dioxide and other green-house gases are, too much of them can bring about undesirable temperature increases, and scientists fear that such increases are occurring on the earth today. Since the start of the Industrial Revolution, human societies have been releasing enormous amounts of carbon dioxide—primarily by burning fossil fuels (coal, oil, and natural gas). Atmospheric concentrations of carbon dioxide have increased by 25%.

As the greenhouse effect would predict, over the past century the global average temperature also has risen—by about 1°F. Most atmospheric scientists believe that excess greenhouse gases already in the atmosphere will bring about an additional 1° to 2°F increase in the next century. Although a 3° temperature increase may not appear to be much of a problem (particularly to inhabitants of colder northern latitudes), this increase is expected to cause radical shifts in global weather—including a significant decrease in rainfall in some of the most important food-producing regions—that would affect human societies throughout the world.

Thus, as important as food, timber, drugs, and other rain-forest products are, they are only the beginning of the many reasons why citizens of industrialized nations rely on tropical rainforests. Just as the plants and animals of the forest are intimately and complexly tied to one another, so too is the rainforest connected to other ecosystems throughout the world. And, like the relationships among the earth's ecosystems, the relationships of living things in the forest are fragile and poorly understood. It is important to keep this in mind, because the destruction of tropical rainforests, in addition to the predicted consequences, may have even more, still-unanticipated repercussions for people living outside the tropics.

More than 12 million acres of tropical forest are logged annually worldwide. Logging and other forms of deforestation are driven by such forces as overpopulation, poverty, and the huge foreign debts of developing tropical nations.

chapter 5

CAUSES OF RAIN-
FOREST DESTRUCTION

Of the many mysteries that still surround rainforests, one of the most basic—and important—questions is: How fast are tropical rainforests disappearing? Experts generally agree that tropical forests of all kinds once covered about 4 billion acres and that roughly half of those forests are gone. Estimates of the current deforestation rate, however, vary widely. Until recently, the most widely accepted figure—29 million acres per year—came from a 1980 study conducted by the United Nations Food and Agriculture Organization (FAO). But more recent studies, summarized in *World Resources 1990–91*, show a much higher rate: up to 51 million acres (an area about the size of Kansas) a year—or 140,000 acres *every day*.

Exactly how fast tropical forests are falling has been vigorously debated for many years. Efforts to find out may seem purely academic, but they are important because both governments and international development agencies that fund forest destruction often use the uncertainty about deforestation rates as an excuse not to protect rainforests. Many scientists, therefore, are calling for an all-out effort to assess global forest cover and deforestation using satellite images combined with ground-level checks to confirm the satellite data. But despite the project's importance, policymakers so far have been unwilling to invest in such a global assessment.

The global deforestation rate is, of course, an average, and in some tropical regions the rate of forest loss is much lower than the average, whereas in others it is skyrocketing. In Costa Rica, the Ivory Coast, and Nigeria, for example, rainforests have been disappearing eight times faster than the currently accepted global average. In Brazil the rate has been even higher. Satellite images showed the loss of 20 million acres in the Amazon Basin alone during 1987, the peak year to date for deforestation in that region. Still, the Amazon remains home to about a third of all tropical rainforests on earth.

Latin America as a whole contains more than half the world's remaining tropical forests, whereas Africa contains about 20% and Asia 24%. The most important causes of deforestation are different in each of these three regions. In general, however, the chief *direct* causes of rainforest loss worldwide are: commercial logging, small- and large-scale agriculture, cattle ranching, and development projects such as hydroelectric dams, roads, and mines. Behind these direct causes are a number of important *indirect* causes of deforestation that, although often left out of discussions about the problem, must also be addressed if rainforests are to survive. These underlying causes include overpopulation, poverty, unequal land distribution, and the huge debts that developing countries owe to industrialized nations.

COMMERCIAL LOGGING AND FUELWOOD

Every year, more than 12 million acres of tropical forest—an area the size of New Hampshire and Vermont—are cut for timber, paper pulp, and other wood products. Although commercial logging does not necessarily have to destroy a forest, careless logging practices often do.

In general, commercial loggers do not clear-cut rainforests; rather, they *selectively* log them. In doing so, they remove between one and five high-value trees per acre and leave the rest of the forest standing. But because those high-value trees are usually the biggest and tallest—and are connected by a tangle of vines to other trees—when they fall, they push or pull their neighbors down with them. Heavy logging machinery also knocks trees down accidentally, and the equipment can compact soil so much that new trees cannot get a start. According to Norman Myers, a typical selective logging enterprise in Southeast Asia "injures beyond repair" one-third to two-thirds of all the trees in a stand.

Commercial logging takes its greatest toll on Southeast Asia's rainforests. According to Malcolm Gillis of Duke University, five-sixths of all tropical hardwoods exported in the 1980s came from Southeast Asia, primarily from Indonesia, Malaysia, and the Philippines. The majority of these exports went to Japan and the United States. In 1982, Indonesia and Malaysia each exported more tropical hardwoods than all Latin American and African countries combined. Indonesia alone, which contains about 10% of the world's tropical forests, logs more than 3 million acres a year.

Tropical hardwood logs are marked and prepared for transport to a mill in Kalimantan, Indonesia. Southeast Asian forests are being logged much faster than they can regenerate.

Because rainforests in these nations are logged much faster than they can regenerate, it is only a matter of time before the forests are depleted. Already, some countries have lost timber markets they once had, and others that currently export timber—the Philippines, in particular—are expected to begin importing wood just to meet their own needs by the end of the 20th century. Despite such grim predictions, commercial logging is accelerating. (In Malaysia, some logging companies are now harvesting trees 24 hours a day, using lights at night.) Logging is fueled partly by developing countries' desperate need for cash to make payments on foreign debts and partly by policies such as those that allow the leasing of forests to corporations or rich individuals who, interested only in short-term profits, care little

continued on page 79

The following pages show some of the many other rainforest inhabitants and their environs. The fate of these species is imperiled by the ongoing destruction of their habitat throughout the tropics.

A two-toed mother sloth, her young pup nestled close, moves exceedingly slowly—and infrequently—from branch to branch in a Panamanian forest.

Besides pleasing the human eye, the beautiful shapes and markings of orchids serve a practical purpose by attracting bird or insect pollinators.

Spreading treetops, vines,
and other flora form
the lush rainforest canopy,
home to the majority
of tropical creatures.

A delicate "cloud forest" flower from a misty,
high-altitude rainforest in Bolivia

The dazzling rufous motmot is found in Panamanian and other neotropical rainforests. When the bird grooms itself, sections of its two long central feathers drop off, exposing the shaft.

One of the better known neotropical rainforest birds is the toucan, recognizable by its huge, colorful bill.

An orangutan in the Tan-
jung Puting National Park
in Kalimantan, Indonesia.
This endangered ape
dwells in the coastal tropical forests of Indonesia,
Brunei, and Malaysia in
Southeast Asia, habitats
that are increasingly
threatened by logging.

An unfortunate leaf katydid—a type
of grasshopper—is devoured by a giant anolis lizard.

This fig-eating bat has
brought a meal to its
roost under a palm leaf.
The animal peels figs
prior to eating them.

An elegantly marked butterfly of the genus Heliconius. There are many thousands of tropical butterfly species.

Spines on this fearsome katydid help protect it from predators—making the insect look to humans like a creature from outer space.

Tree frogs climb aided by tiny suction disks on their feet.

The brilliant coloring of the poison dart frog warns potential predators that the skin of this tiny amphibian contains lethal toxins.

continued from page 70

about the long-term welfare of the forests. As Southeast Asia's share of the international market in tropical timber falls—as experts agree it will—the logging of African and Latin American rainforests will intensify.

In many tropical regions, people also harvest rainforest trees to use as fuel for heating their homes and cooking their food. Although it is a more serious problem in dry tropical forests, fuelwood gathering takes a tremendous toll in certain rainforested areas, including southern Mexico and some parts of Central America. Worldwide, more than two-thirds of the inhabitants of developing countries rely almost entirely on wood for heating and cooking.

SUBSISTENCE AGRICULTURE

More than 20 million acres of tropical rainforest, an area about the size of South Carolina, are cleared each year to make way for farms. This major cause of rainforest destruction is often closely tied to logging. When commercial loggers open up a previously inaccessible forest by building roads, hordes of poor, landless farmers follow these roads into the forest, cut down trees the loggers left behind, and plant crops. Although each individual clears only enough land to feed a family, the collective damage caused by this subsistence farming is enormous. According to the FAO, more than half of all logged forests eventually are cleared by once-landless farmers hoping for a better life.

Sadly, most of these farmers' hopes are quickly dashed. As discussed in chapter 2, rainforest soils are different from those that support temperate forests in that most of them are poor in nutrients. The nutrients instead are stored in living trees and other plants. When rainforests are cleared, the nitrogen, phosphorous, and other nutrients bound up in the vegetation may initially flush into the soil, but they quickly wash away in harsh tropical rains. Soon, the land becomes infertile. Within three or four growing seasons, crops fail, and poor farmers—who cannot afford expensive chemical fertilizers—are forced to move on and clear more rainforest.

But rainforest soils are not incapable of supporting crops. For thousands of years, rainforests have been farmed successfully by longtime residents, primarily indigenous groups, using a technique known as shifting cultivation. Also called slash-and-burn agriculture, this ancient practice involves first clearing a small forest plot by cutting the vegetation and burning it, which provides ashes to fertilize the soil. This plot is farmed for several seasons, until its nutrients are depleted, then left alone to recover while the farmer clears another small plot. Within about 30 years, the original plot reverts to forest, and the farmer may clear it again. As practiced traditionally, shifting cultivation allows food to be grown sustainably over a long period of time by keeping the land productive.

But today overpopulation and the tremendous influx of new rainforest immigrants are causing this traditional system to break down. The pressure of too many people on too little land forces farmers to clear plots that are larger than they should be and to return to those plots before they have had a chance to recover. The result is permanently degraded land that can support neither crops nor new forest. The loss of nutrients is not the only barrier to recovery. When too much forest is lost, the birds, insects, and other animals that pollinate and disperse the seeds of rainforest trees also are wiped out, and the surviving trees cannot reproduce. And even if a seed does manage to sprout, the high heat, low humidity, and bright light of a forest clearing will kill most rainforest seedlings, which are adapted to the cooler, more humid conditions of the forest interior.

RANCHING AND EXPORT CROPS

If subsistence farmers are turning rainforest into wasteland, the impact of large-scale commercial agriculture—particularly cattle ranching—is even more severe. Throughout

Amazon forest burns in Rondônia, Brazil. Fires are set to clear land for farming and ranching, but infertile rainforest soils are quickly degraded.

the tropics, vast tracts of forest have been completely leveled to make way for huge plantations of single crops grown for export. In different regions, different crops dominate. In Southeast Asia, for example, rubber, cacao, and palm oil are the major export crops, whereas in Central America, coffee, bananas, and sugarcane are predominant.

Another export, beef, is often more damaging than these crops, both because cattle ranching requires clearing more forest than does cultivation of most other crops and because the animals, whose hooves trample and compact soil, are particularly hard on the land. Each year, cattle ranching destroys about 5 million acres of tropical rainforest, mostly in Latin America. Between 1950 and 1980, the area of cattle pasture in Central America (most of it from cleared rainforest) doubled, as did the number of beef cattle. Beef exports, primarily to the United States, increased nearly fivefold. Most of the beef imported by the United States during this period went into pet foods and fast-food hamburgers. Today more U.S. beef comes from New Zealand and Australia, and most Central American beef is either consumed there or exported to Europe.

Cattle ranches carved out of rainforest are no more sustainable than are most agricultural fields. According to Myers, both soil fertility and the proportion of grass species that cattle will eat decline appreciably after five years. Within 10 years, many pastures become completely useless and are abandoned by ranchers, who must move on and clear more forest.

Given the inefficiency of this system, why is it that more farmers do not give up cattle ranching and switch to fruit and vegetable crops? One reason is that although ranches may fail in the end, they last longer—and cost less to set up—than do plantations of most other crops. Beef also tends to fetch higher prices in international markets and is less subject to the ups and downs of market demand than are products such as coffee, bananas, and sugarcane.

Perhaps the most important reason why cattle ranching has thrived in Latin America is that some governments have actively promoted the industry. Until recently, the Brazilian government, for example, provided generous tax credits, subsidies, and income tax breaks to wealthy ranchers who made profits by buying and selling land, even though their ranches went broke. They sold their land after inflation increased its value and wrote off their ranch losses against other sources of income. Even at best, large cattle ranches benefit few people besides their owners. Ranches take up huge tracts of land that could be devoted to other crops. They also employ few people and provide little in the way of food or income to rural communities.

MEGA–DEVELOPMENT PROJECTS

Aided by international lending institutions such as the World Bank, governments of developing countries that mount huge development projects, such as hydroelectric dams, mines, and road networks, often have only the best intentions: providing energy, jobs, and economic development to poor, rural regions. Too often, however, these schemes end up hurting more people than they help, and they destroy huge tracts of rainforest in the process.

The construction of hydroelectric dams is a case in point. Intended to provide inexpensive sources of energy for rural people and to promote industrial development, large dams flood thousands of square miles of forest, displacing plants, animals, and human settlements—usually of indigenous people. On Amazonia's Uatumá River, for instance, the Balbina Dam alone flooded 900 square miles of forest and forced thousands of people from their homes. Brazil is currently planning dozens of other large dams throughout the Amazon.

These hydroelectric dams generally do succeed in attracting industry. However, much of the industrial development that has sprung up around dams has been environmentally unsound. In the Amazon basin, the largest industrial project so far, the Grande Carajás, began around a dam 10 years ago to exploit the region's large deposits of iron ore, copper, manganese, nickel, bauxite, and gold. Today the mining project covers 324,000 square miles, more than 10% of Brazil's entire land area, or an area larger than Texas. So far, the most damaging part of the Grande Carajás project is an iron ore mine. Although the mine itself has not destroyed much forest, four smelters (facilities used to melt down iron ore to pig iron) are fueled by charcoal made from rainforest trees; 25 new smelters are now planned. Tree plantations may someday meet a portion of this need for wood, but most of it will continue to come from the forest. According to the World Bank, which helped finance the project, more than a million tons of charcoal a year will be needed, requiring the clearing of between 1.4 million and 3 million acres of rainforest.

The Brazilian government has long sought to draw both industry and settlers to the Amazon—in part to establish a strong Brazilian presence in parts of the country near its borders and in part to relieve human suffering in poor, overcrowded regions. In addition to building dams and offering economic incentives to ranchers, the government has attracted colonists to the Amazon by constructing vast networks of roads throughout this once-inaccessible wilderness. Between 1981 and 1983, for example, the World Bank loaned Brazil more than $400 million to promote colonization and economic development in the states of Rondônia and Mato Grosso. Most of the money went into the paving of a road, BR-364, that brought more than 200,000 landless farmers into the region in 1989 alone. Unfortunately, as in rainforests throughout the world, many of these migrants' farms failed within a few years, forcing them to move on. In Brazil, immigrants also have become involved in bloody battles over land rights with both indigenous groups, who have long occupied the area, and with wealthy cattle ranchers who have arrived recently.

In Indonesia, the government's wish to move people to sparsely populated parts of the country has turned into the world's largest official resettlement program. Dubbed the transmigration program, the scheme seeks to reduce the population of crowded islands such as Java and Bali by encouraging people to move to rainforested islands such as Borneo, Sumatra, and New Guinea. Between 1950 and 1979, the government sponsored about 828,000 migrants through the program, and between 1979 and 1986—with a World Bank loan of $500 million—it moved nearly 1.5 million more. Officials have disagreed on the success of the program: Although some farms have succeeded, many have failed as a result of the poor soils and disorganized administration of the program. However, there is little disagreement on the impact the program has had on the region's rainforests: the environmental organization Friends of the Earth estimates that between 1984 and 1989 alone, at least 7.44 million acres were lost.

A new road built in Indonesia will transport loggers and farmers into the rainforest. Many development projects in tropical nations prove unsustainable, destroying forests without significantly alleviating economic problems.

ROOT CAUSES OF DEFORESTATION

A farmer clearing a small plot to grow corn; a rancher burning hundreds of acres to create a cattle pasture; a logger wielding a powerful chain saw that, in minutes, topples a 100-year-old tree; these are the obvious causes of tropical deforestation. But behind these visible causes are several powerful forces that leave the person holding the machete, match, or chain saw little other choice. If these behind-the-scenes problems are not solved, no plan to save the world's rainforests can ever succeed.

The first of these problems is overpopulation. The earth's human population, which doubled in less than 40 years to reach

5 billion in 1987, is still growing by about 90 million per year. More than 90% of this population growth is taking place in tropical Asia, Africa, and Latin America. As the populations of these developing nations soar, rainforests come under increasing pressure to provide people with more and more land, food, and products to sell for cash. Not surprisingly, in Africa and Latin America, the countries that have the highest population growth rates also have the highest deforestation rates.

Tropical developing countries also tend to be the world's poorest. Forty percent of the developing world's population— about 1.2 billion people—lives in abject poverty. Two-thirds of these people eat fewer than 90% of the calories needed to lead a normal, active life. Throughout the tropics, more than 14 million children and 1 million elderly people starve to death each year. The poorest people of all live in urban slums or rural areas that are often near tropical forests. Struggling just to make it from one day to the next, many of these people are forced to cut down rainforests to grow food or scour the forests for something they can eat or sell.

The wealth that does exist in tropical nations tends to be concentrated in the hands of very few individuals. Land, in particular, is unfairly distributed. In Latin America, just 7% of all landowners control 93% of the land that is suitable for growing crops. About 20 million Latin Americans have no land at all or have too little to grow enough food to feed their families. With the best lands taken up mainly by cattle ranches and export crops, landless farmers often have no choice other than to try to farm the rainforest.

That vast areas of tropical nations' farmlands are occupied by export crops—rather than by crops that could feed the native population—is no accident. The majority of these countries are deeply in debt, and they badly need cash to make interest payments on those debts. During the 1970s and 1980s, many developing countries borrowed heavily from industrialized nations and from institutions such as the World Bank in order to invest in projects that would spur much-needed economic growth. But when higher oil prices and interest rates and a global recession struck, these countries were unable to pay back their loans. Together the developing nations owe about $1 trillion. Some of the nations most deeply in debt are those that are rich in rainforests. Brazil, for example—which contains three-fifths of the Amazon, the world's largest rainforest—owed about $115 billion in 1989 and spent nearly 42% of its export earnings on debt pay-

A slum in Iquitos, Peru, a city bordering the Amazon River. Widespread poverty and overpopulation in the tropics are major underlying causes of rainforest destruction.

ments. These financial pressures have encouraged tropical countries to rapidly exploit their rainforests for timber or to cut them down to produce cattle or so-called cash crops for export.

The role that foreign debts play in tropical deforestation clearly demonstrates that the world's industrialized nations are not merely innocent bystanders to the problem. Not only do the inhabitants of industrialized countries depend on rainforests in many ways, but they also, willingly or not, play a role in their destruction. When people of the temperate zone first hear about tropical deforestation, their first impulse is to boycott rainforest products. But solutions to this complicated problem are not so simple. In many cases, the citizens of industrialized nations could help more by *buying* certain tropical products—as long as they are produced sustainably—and by convincing their governments to provide relief from the debts that drive tropical nations to sell off their rainforests for fast cash.

A portion of rainforest in the Amazon basin bears the scars of slash-and-burn agriculture.

chapter 6

CONSEQUENCES OF DEFORESTATION

The potential of tropical rainforests to provide humanity with food, pharmaceuticals, building materials, natural pesticides, and other products has barely been tapped—yet already these forests have provided hundreds of such essentials. The possible loss of these and still-to-be-discovered products is one of the major reasons given for protecting rainforests. To many people, however, the loss of products that bear little resemblance to their rainforest source is not a compelling reason to act on behalf of the forests. The potential loss of still-unknown products is even harder for people to become concerned about, as are some of the other consequences of deforestation—such as changes in climate, water cycles, and numbers of species—that are still surrounded by uncertainty.

To be thoroughly convinced of the seriousness of the deforestation crisis, however, one need only look at parts of the world that have suffered heavy rainforest losses. In these regions, the predicted dire consequences of deforestation—including the loss of economy-sustaining export products, the disruption of hydrologic cycles, and the decimation of indigenous cultures and species—are already taking place. They provide an ominous hint of what the future will hold throughout the tropics unless deforestation slows or stops.

THE FOREST FOR THE TREES

Already, several tropical nations that once relied on timber products for essential export revenue have lost those valuable markets. In Nigeria, for example, annual timber exports declined from approximately 1 million cubic yards in 1964 to fewer than 130,000 cubic yards in recent years. Between 1974 and 1985, Ghana's timber exports fell by two-thirds. Today neither of these nations holds an important share of the world timber market, and their stories may soon be repeated elsewhere. One study has predicted that if current trends continue, fewer than 10 of the 33 nations that now export tropical hardwoods will continue to do so by the year 2000. These export losses, which in most cases could be avoided by more careful, sustainable logging practices, represent the loss of foreign exchange that countries desperately need to feed, clothe, house, and otherwise care for their burgeoning populations.

A loss that will hit the people of the tropics even more directly is the dwindling supply of the fuelwood they use to cook their food and heat their homes. In many of the areas where it is needed most, fuelwood has become scarce. In the early 1980s, about half of the 2 billion people who depended on wood for cooking and heating could not find enough, and the rest were forced to overexploit fuelwood sources. Although this problem is more common in tropical dry-forest regions—particularly western

Africa and parts of Asia—fuelwood shortages also afflict some rainforest regions, including parts of Central America and Mexico.

In areas facing fuelwood shortages, the search for wood dominates the lives of poor families, particularly women and children, who must spend many hours each day scouring the countryside for wood. When they are unable to find enough, they are forced to turn to substitutes, primarily animal manure and crop residues. But burning these wastes robs croplands of the only fertilizers available in poor, rural areas. Every year, an estimated 400 million tons of manure are burned for fuel in developing countries. If used instead to fertilize fields, this manure could raise grain production by 20 million tons.

WATER: TOO LITTLE, TOO MUCH

The important role that rainforests play in tempering the impact of erratic tropical rainfall has become all too clear in regions that have suffered heavy deforestation. Without the forest's "sponge" to soak up and store water, releasing it gradually to surrounding land and bodies of water, many tropical regions today face periodic water shortages that threaten life-sustaining staple crops. In Thailand, the Philippines, Indonesia, and other Southeast Asian countries, farmers periodically cannot get enough irrigation water to ensure successful rice crops. In 1977–78, one drought in heavily deforested peninsular Malaysia caused the nation to lose more than a quarter of its rice harvest.

Ironically, many of these same countries face devastating floods during the rainy season. These disasters, too, are caused by the loss of forests that once protected the land from the full force of harsh tropical rains. In 1981, for example, 331,000 people in

A young girl uses a makeshift outdoor sink on an eroded hillside in Costa Rica. Landless farmers often have little choice but to try to farm the rainforest.

the Philippines—a severely deforested nation—had to be evacuated because of flooding. Damage to crops, livestock, and buildings totaled $30 million. The disaster led then-president Ferdinand Marcos to declare deforestation a national emergency.

Seven years later, similar flooding hit Thailand. This country, which as recently as 1950 was two-thirds forested, today has rainforests covering just one-fifth of its land area. The 1988 flooding followed heavy rains that pounded deforested hillsides, causing water and mud to pour down onto the villages below, completely burying some of them. More than 400 people died, and thousands more were left homeless. Following the flood, Thailand became the first developing country to ban commercial logging (although rubber plantations and subsistence farming have been responsible for as much, if not more, of the nation's deforestation).

As unchecked rainwater rushes down deforested slopes, it carries away precious topsoil and leaves the land too damaged to produce either crops or new forest. Today this soil erosion is a serious problem in many tropical nations that have lost large areas of rainforest. In the Cauca Valley watershed of Colombia, for example, 20 tons of soil per acre were lost from deforested hillsides over a period of just 10 months. In heavily deforested Madagascar, up to 130 tons of soil per acre are lost each year. By contrast, U.S. croplands lose between five and six tons of soil per year. The Indonesian island of Java, which has just 15% of its original forest left, loses about 770 million tons of topsoil from all its croplands annually.

In addition to rendering the land unsuitable for crops or forest, soil erosion wreaks havoc with dams, shipping canals, and the natural ecosystems where eroded topsoil eventually is deposited. Throughout the tropics, eroded soils are filling up the reservoirs of hydroelectric dams with silt, cutting many years from the dams' useful lives. In the Philippines, the Ambuklao Dam, which was expected to last 56 years, will probably be silted up in 32 years. In Pakistan, the Mangla Dam has lost about 50 of its 100 years of potential use, and in Costa Rica siltation of the Cachi Dam will mean the loss of between $133 million and $274 million in revenues.

Sediments are also clogging up shipping canals. In 1977, for example, a combination of sedimentation and drought lowered water levels in the Panama Canal (located in a region that has suffered heavy deforestation) so much that ships could not get through and had to be diverted an extra 11,615 miles around

Cape Horn. When eroded soils are eventually dumped into the sea, they cause problems there as well. Throughout the tropics, coral reefs are being smothered by sediments deposited by rivers. Worldwide, rivers discharge approximately 13 billion tons of sediment into the oceans each year. More than half comes from rivers flowing out of tropical South America and Asia.

LOSS OF INDIGENOUS CULTURES

A good number of the rainforests that loggers, miners, farmers, and cattle ranchers invade are already inhabited. For eons, forest-dwelling peoples have lived throughout the world's tropics. For the most part, such indigenous groups live in harmony with their environment, having devised a variety of ways to

Cattle ranching is a growing threat to rainforests and their native inhabitants. Besides destroying the land itself, ranchers and other settlers bring diseases into the forest and often kill people who try to stand in their way.

sustain themselves while ensuring the long-term health of the forests on which they rely, as described in chapter 4.

But today most of these indigenous peoples are being decimated. When rainforests are destroyed, their inhabitants lose not only their homes but also their food and other means of survival. Often, colonists deliberately kill native people in fierce battles over land. In most cases, such massacres occur with the full knowledge of the government, and sometimes the removal of indigenous groups from rainforests is officially sanctioned.

"Modern states, and the citizens who hold power in them, covet land and resources that have long been managed by indigenous peoples," writes anthropologist Jason W. Clay, of the organization Cultural Survival, in *Lessons of the Rainforest.* "The states and individuals who can ultimately claim control of these resources stand to gain considerably; and since they have the power to do so, they persecute and kill the indigenous peoples who stand in their way." In some places, notably Amazonia, governments have encouraged white settlers to take over in-digenous lands in order to bolster their nation's claim to dis-puted territory. In the Brazilian Amazon, the construction of government-sponsored hydroelectric dams has flooded thousands of acres of tribal lands, and the industry and settlers attracted by these dams have killed off game animals and polluted native peoples' water supplies.

Even worse than this direct assault has been the in-advertent introduction of diseases by white settlers. Long isolated from the rest of the world, indigenous peoples have not had an opportunity to develop resistance to such common illnesses as influenza, whooping cough, tuberculosis, and measles. These diseases, therefore, are usually fatal and are killing thousands of native forest inhabitants worldwide. Over the past 3 years, one Amazonian tribe, the Yanomami, has lost 1 in 10 members to diseases brought in by whites.

The largest forest tribe remaining in the neotropics, the Yanomami's story is typical. Until recently, these people, numbering more than 20,000, had been living in northern Brazil and southern Venezuela in much the same fashion as they had for generations—hunting, gathering, and farming without damaging the forest. But beginning in the late 1980s, thousands of gold miners from other parts of Brazil invaded Yanomami territory. By 1990, the miners, whose ranks had swelled to more than 100,000, had polluted the region's rivers, driven away wildlife, introduced deadly diseases (including hepatitis, tuberculosis, influenza, and new strains of malaria), and killed off scores of native people in battles over food and land. Without the fish and game on which they relied, many Yanomami have been forced to beg for food from the same people who destroyed those precious resources. Although the miners' invasion of Yanomami lands has been declared illegal and the government has made a few attempts to evict them, in early 1991 the miners were still firmly entrenched, and the number of Yanomami was continuing to drop rapidly.

If the past serves as any indication of the future, complete extinction of the Yanomami people is a definite possibility. When Europeans first came to the Brazilian Amazon in the 16th century, more than 6 million indigenous people inhabited these forests. Today fewer than 250,000 remain. According to Cultural Survival, one indigenous group has died out in Brazil every year since 1900. And even when indigenous people are lucky enough to escape with their lives, deforestation inevitably pushes them into small reserves or forces them to integrate into the dominant white society and to give up their traditional ways of life.

SPECIES EXTINCTIONS

As discussed earlier, of the 1.4 million plant and animal species that have been named and described by scientists to date, at least half live in the world's tropical rainforests. Biologists believe that millions more species remain to be discovered, most of them in the tropics. Yet scientists also agree that the planet is losing vast numbers of rainforest species. They claim that the earth today is in the midst of a huge "extinction spasm" that is greater than any extinction episode that has occurred since the dinosaurs and their kin disappeared 65 million years ago.

How many rainforest species is the world losing? To answer this question, biologists use a set of principles from the

A dam reservoir in the Ivory Coast, Africa. Large hydroelectric dams flood thousands of acres of rainforest, displacing indigenous peoples and destroying wildlife habitat.

theory of island biogeography, which was proposed by E. O. Wilson of Harvard University and Robert MacArthur of Princeton in the late 1960s. The theory states that the number of species that can exist on an island—either an actual oceanic island or a habitat island such as a forest that is isolated from other forests—is a function of the island's size, the amount of time it has been isolated, and the distance to the nearest "mainland" (in the case of a forest, the closest large forest of the same kind). The smaller an island—or forest—is, the longer it has been isolated; the farther it is from a mainland, the fewer species it can support.

Using these principles, ecologist Walter Reid of the World Resources Institute has estimated that if current deforestation rates continue, by 2020 the tropical forests of Asia, Africa, and South America will lose up to 17% of their species. If the deforestation rate doubles, Asia could lose half its species. Some scientists say that by 2050 a quarter of all species on earth could vanish. Assuming that 10 million plant and animal species inhabit the planet (a conservative estimate), this projection means that 15,000 to 50,000 species are becoming extinct in the tropics each year—or 50 to 150 species *every day*.

As bad as these estimates sound, some experts believe the situation is even worse, at least in some particularly hard-hit rainforests. According to Norman Myers, the extinction rate will soon skyrocket in 10 tropical forest regions: Madagascar, the Atlantic coast of Brazil, western Ecuador, the Colombian Chocó, the uplands of western Amazonia, the eastern Himalayas, peninsular Malaysia, northern Borneo, the Philippines, and New Caledonia. In these extinction "hotspots," says Myers, 34,000 plant species and at least 700,000 animal species are threatened by deforestation rates much higher than the global average. He fears that within the next decade these areas will lose 90% of their remaining forests—and approximately 350,000 species. According to Myers, this loss will represent the "greatest single setback to life's abundance and diversity since the first flickerings of life almost 4 billion years ago."

Beyond the sheer number of species that are vanishing, the nature of today's extinction spasm has many scientists worried. In the extinction episode that wiped out the dinosaurs, most mammals, birds, amphibians, and many reptiles survived. But today all kinds of animals are being affected. Most plants survived all five of the earth's major extinctions, yet today they too are succumbing.

As with most other consequences of tropical deforestation, the full extent of species extinction remains unknown. As stated in chapter 2, scientists do not yet know how many species live on the earth. Most estimates run between 5 million and 30 million, with only a tiny fraction of the total discovered so far. How many of these species will vanish forever before scientists even know what they are? Which of these plants and animals will turn out to be essential components of the rainforest ecosystem? Which of them contain chemicals that might provide a cure for cancer? Unfortunately, these answers may not be known until it is much too late.

FOREST DWELLERS FIGHTING TO SAVE THEIR HOMES

Not surprisingly, some of the most inspiring battles to save rainforests are being fought by the forests' indigenous peoples. Unlike the inhabitants of distant temperate nations, or even of big cities in the tropics—all of whom experience the loss of rainforests in an abstract way—the forests' native peoples are truly losing everything: their homes, their means of livelihood, their culture, and their lives.

In the Amazon, some of the most successful struggles have been waged by the Kayapó, an Indian nation of 8,500 people living in the Brazilian state of Pará. Following ancient traditions, the Kayapó make their living by hunting, fishing, farming, and gathering wild plants. But in recent years, their way of life has been increasingly threatened as gold miners, ranchers, and other outsiders haved moved into Kayapó territory, taking over land and replacing ancient traditions.

The Kayapó are fighting hard to keep their lands and culture. Over the past eight years, the group has organized demonstrations in the state capital, driven illegal settlers off its land, and closed down two gold mines illegally operating in Kayapó territory. But their most impressive victory came in 1988, when two Kayapó leaders went to Washington, D.C., to protest a proposed World Bank–funded dam that would have flooded 2,000 square miles of Amazonian forest and displaced 70,000 people. After meeting with the Kayapó leaders, the bank decided to postpone its $500,000 loan.

Less lucky than the Kayapó are the Dayak, indigenous people who live in the rainforests of Borneo. For many years, Dayak tribes throughout this Indonesian island lost their lands and traditions when commercial loggers destroyed their forests. To survive, many had no choice but to go to work for the logging companies.

But one Dayak tribe, the Penan, has not given up so easily. The Penan, who live in the state of Sarawak in the Malaysian part of Borneo, are among the world's last true hunter-gatherers, hunting game with blowpipes and poison arrows and collecting wild plants. Already, one-third of the Penan's forests have been logged, and about five square miles are still logged each day. To protest the destruction, tribe members have been forming human blockades across logging roads. More than a hundred Penan have been arrested in the protests, and thousands of letters have been sent to the Malaysian government—and to Japan, which buys most of Malaysia's timber exports—supporting the Penan's cause. Although the government has not yet changed its policies toward rainforests, the Penan plan to fight on. As a statement prepared by one group arrested in 1989 puts it, "We love our land and forest, which our forefathers gave to us, very much. We don't want to leave this land."

A Kayapó chief and 350 other Indian leaders converge on Brazil's capital in 1989, hoping to meet with President José Sarney to protest the invasion of gold miners in the Amazon.

Countries both within and outside the tropics are responsible for rain-forest destruction, and the cooperation of all is needed to slow this devastation.

S O L U T I O N S

Can anything be done to save the world's tropical rainforests? Fortunately, there are a number of ways to protect the forests, and governments, conservation organizations, businesses, and citizens around the world are now engaged in a great many of these activities. The recent groundswell of public concern for rainforests has provided new sources of funding for many of these projects. Although such developments certainly provide a reason for optimism, that 50 million acres of rainforest still vanish every year means that far more action is needed on all fronts.

F O R E S T   P A R K S   A N D   R E S E R V E S

One of the most obvious—and most important—approaches to saving rainforests is to protect them in national parks, the same way that industrialized nations such as the United States and Canada safeguard their natural wonders. Yet so far fewer than 5% of the world's tropical forests are included in parks or other kinds of protected areas. Most of the developing countries that house these forests simply do not have enough money to buy land and set up park systems. And many of the nations that do establish parks are then unable to pay park rangers to protect the land. These unprotected parks routinely are invaded by poor, local people who desperately need the forest's wood, food, land, or products to sell. The areas are often called "paper parks" because they exist on paper but not in reality.

Fortunately, as recognition of this problem has grown in recent years, there has been a revolution in the way governments and conservationists plan parks and other pro-tected areas. Instead of making parks into fortresses that shut out all people—except tourists—park designers in developing countries now try to integrate local people into the park as much as possible and to allow them at least limited use of its natural resources.

The most widely used model for this new breed of park is the *biosphere reserve* developed by the United Nations Educational, Scientific, and Cultural Organization (UNESCO). Unlike traditional parks, biosphere reserves include rather than exclude people. The typical reserve is divided into several different zones, sometimes arranged concentrically around one another. At the center is a strictly protected area called the core zone, in which only activities such as environmental monitoring and research are allowed. Beyond this zone lies a buffer zone that allows a variety of activities, including education and training, nature tourism, and traditional kinds of land use, such as hunting and gathering, as long as they are compatible with the protection of the core. At the edge of the reserve is the final zone, the transition zone, where communities of people actually live—farming, fishing, and making their living in ways that do not jeopardize the long-term health of the forest. These people, who begin to rely on the reserve for both their income and the essentials of life, often become the forest's most important defenders.

Costa Rica, more than any other rainforested nation, has embraced these new concepts of park management. Recently, for example, the government organized its parks and other protected areas into nine regional conservation units that include both strictly protected zones and zones where local people may live and use natural resources. The conservation units are intended to promote rural development as well as conservation. Costa Rica also has set aside an impressive number of protected areas, which encompass some 3.4 million acres, or 27% of its national territory. These parks safeguard a significant amount of Costa Rica's—and the world's—biological diversity. In an area about the size of West Virginia, this nation has more bird species than the United States and Canada combined and twice as many plant species as California, which is 18 times larger.

Although the impetus for protecting this nation's rainforests and biological diversity has come from Costa Ricans themselves, one reason the government can justify its investments in national parks is that foreign tourists have increasingly been willing to pay to visit these areas. Worldwide, such natural-history-oriented travel to remote parts of the world—or ecotourism—is a booming business that is providing many tropical nations with new incentives to protect rainforests. Costa Rica is one of the most popular ecotourism sites: In 1980 about 60,000 U.S. citizens went to the country—primarily to visit its national parks. By 1988 the number had grown to 102,000, a 70% increase in just 8 years.

But as helpful as ecotourism dollars are, they are still a drop in the bucket when it comes to what tropical nations need to purchase and protect rainforest reserves. To help generate some of this badly needed income, conservation organizations have been devising creative new fund-raising strategies. By far the most innovative idea to date is the so-called *debt-for-nature swap*. In these swaps, a conservation group buys part of a developing country's foreign debt from a bank (at a discount, because the bank has little hope of ever collecting the full amount). The group then remits the debt to the debtor nation's central bank, which converts it to local currency and invests the money in conser- vation. Organizations such as the World Wildlife Fund Conservation International, and The Nature Conservancy have participated in debt-for-nature swaps in several countries— including Costa Rica, Bolivia, Ecuador, and the Philippines—that have resulted in millions of dollars being spent to purchase and manage rainforest reserves.

Foreign tourists meet native villagers in Orejón, Peru. Tourism provides much-needed cash for tropical nations and encourages them to preserve their forests in national parks.

AGRICULTURE: GETTING MORE FOR LESS

As important as rainforest reserves are, even the best-managed protected areas are not safe if their human neighbors cannot feed themselves and their children. One of the major reasons that rainforests are cleared today is to make way for crops—both for local consumption and for cash to buy food and other goods. As the populations of developing tropical nations continue to grow rapidly, so will the demand for even more food and cash crops. One way to reduce agriculture's pressure on *primary* (never-before-cut) rainforests is to encourage farmers to plant crops and raise livestock on other lands such as grasslands, *secondary* (previously cut) forests, and abandoned farm- and ranchlands.

But even more critical than finding alternative land to farm is finding ways to grow more food on less land—and with less damage to the land and surrounding forests. Agricultural experts agree that the key to accomplishing both of these goals—as well as to making farms sustainable—is to use farming practices that mimic diverse natural systems whenever possible. Most modern agricultural systems, however, are the very antithesis of nature: gigantic *monocultures*—fields of a single kind of crop—that drain the soil of nutrients and attract pests and therefore do not run without expensive chemical fertilizers and pesticides.

There are many steps that farmers can take to make their farms more like natural ecosystems—and therefore more environmentally sound. One is to cultivate small, rather than large, plots and to preserve as much forest as possible around the fields.

Another improvement would be to plant diverse crops to-gether—in a *polyculture*—and to include, especially, plants that help others out. There are, for instance, nitrogen-fixing plants whose roots host fungi that convert nitrogen into a form that other plants can use, thereby providing a natural fertilizer. Other plants provide homes to beneficial insects that prey on pests, supplying crops with a natural insecticide.

Throughout the tropics, farmers following both ancient traditions and modern innovations are already taking many of these steps. In northern Mexico and parts of Central America, for example, Lacandon Maya Indians, farming much the same way their ancestors did, create *milpas*, small forest plots that support up to 80 different crops a year. Highly productive, one milpa smaller than two acres produces two and a quarter metric tons of corn and an equal amount of root and tree crops in a year.

In Java, Indonesia, farmers plant home gardens, known as pekarangan, that feature a variety of crops grown in layers much like those of a natural rainforest: a ground layer of vegetables such as beans, spinach, tomatoes, and medicinal plants; an understory layer of banana, papaya, and cassava; a canopy layer of coffee, cacao, and fruit trees; and even an emergent layer made up of tall trees such as the coconut palm. Javanese farmers care-fully save leaf litter and other wastes from the pekarangan and use the materials to fertilize the soil. These tiny agricultural forests are both highly efficient and productive, providing up to 25% of a family's income and 40% of its calories.

In some rainforested regions, particularly Latin America, the most destructive agricultural activity is cattle ranching. Work-ing first in Panama and later in Costa Rica, scientists from the Smithsonian Tropical Research Institute are offering some Latin

Americans a more efficient and less destructive alternative: ranching green iguanas. Iguanas are a traditional source of protein throughout this region, but most of their natural populations have been depleted by overhunting. After perfecting techniques for breeding and raising the reptiles in captivity, researchers had farmers test iguana ranching in unfenced forests. So far, the experiment has been a success: The iguanas are producing the same amount of—and in some cases more—protein per acre as cattle, and it costs much less to feed the reptiles. Even more .important, iguana ranching does not require rainforest destruction; in fact, because the animals feed on the leaves of forest trees and plants, the iguana ranches have provided rural people with a good reason *not* to cut down their forests.

IMPROVING FOREST MANAGEMENT

One way to lessen the toll of commercial logging on primary rainforests would be to establish more tree farms, or plantations, of valuable rainforest species. Harvesting more wood from secondary forests also would reduce pressure on primary forests. According to Myers, there are enough of these younger, disturbed forests today to produce all the industrial wood the world will need from tropical forests until the year 2000.

But even if the pressure of commercial logging on primary rainforests can be lessened, these forests will continue to be exploited for their valuable hardwoods, many of which do not occur in disturbed forests and cannot be grown on plantations. Given that reality, much can still be done to reduce logging's impact. As discussed in chapter 5, although the timber industry tends to selectively harvest only the most valuable rainforest species, logging operations damage one-third to two-thirds of the trees left behind—and thus severely degrade the entire forest.

Yet selective logging *can* be practiced sustainably. To lessen its damage, loggers could take a few extra steps, such as cutting down the lianas that connect one tree to another before harvesting the target tree and making sure the tree falls in a direction that does the least damage to its neighbors. Loggers could also remove logs from the forest with lighter machinery, which compacts the soil less (even helicopters have been used experimentally in Borneo) and leaves behind branches, bark, and leaves that, when they decompose, would return nutrients to the soil. These changes could make the final product more expensive. But environmentalists hope that conscientious consumers will be willing to spend a little bit more for tropical timber products that were obtained using ecologically sound methods.

One barrier to the adoption of these reforms is that most timber companies harvesting rainforests today have no stake in the long-term survival—or even profitability—of those forests. In most tropical nations, governments own the majority of rainforest lands but lease them to private companies, either national or international, for logging. Because most leases are for short periods of time—between 5 and 10 years—timber companies have no incentive to harvest trees carefully, preferring to take the most valuable trees right away for a quick profit and then move on to a new forest. To force companies to be more responsible, many experts recommend that tropical nations charge more money for logging concessions and make the leases longer—at least 70 years—so timber companies are motivated to preserve the forest through more than one harvesting cycle.

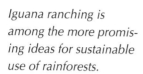
Iguana ranching is among the more promising ideas for sustainable use of rainforests.

Another way to lessen the toll of commercial logging on rainforests is for tropical nations to manage those forests for products other than wood. As pointed out in chapter 4, rainforests provide a wealth of commercially important products in addition to wood, including food, drugs, oils, fibers, and rubber. A recent study in the Peruvian Amazon showed that selling these nonwood products in local markets generates two to three times more income than either harvesting the forest's trees or cutting them down for cattle ranches. Some governments are finally beginning to pay attention to these facts. Spurred in part by publicity surrounding the assassination of celebrated rubber tapper Chico Mendes, the Brazilian government has established 10 million acres of *extractive reserves*, forest reserves that are protected for and managed by local people who make their living harvesting rubber, Brazil nuts, fruits, and other nontimber products that require preservation of intact rainforests.

Some businesses are helping to make such efforts more profitable. Vermont's Ben & Jerry's Homemade Ice Cream, Inc., for example, has developed a new flavor, Rainforest Crunch, that features Brazil nuts and cashews harvested from the wild; the company is planning other new flavors based on exotic rainforest fruits. The Body Shop, a British cosmetics chain, is buying Amazonian herbs for a new line of rainforest cosmetics. Cultural Survival's Jason Clay, who works with these companies and is a major supporter of their approach to saving rainforests, says: "We want to show that a living rain forest makes more money than a dead rain forest."

Fruits, nuts, and other nonwood rainforest products can be harvested profitably, and goods containing them are increasingly popular with environmentally conscious consumers.

"GREENING" THE DEVELOPMENT BANKS

Some of the most massive rainforest losses occur when developing tropical nations launch huge development projects—such as hydroelectric dams that flood hundreds of square miles of forest or road networks that open previously inaccessible forests to industry and settlement. Before proceeding with any of these expensive projects, the governments of developing countries must first obtain loans from wealthy lending organizations: the World Bank or regional banks such as the Inter-American Development Bank. Together these institutions loan 151 countries more than $25 billion a year. More than half of these loans go to projects that directly affect tropical forests, usually in a negative way.

Until recently, decisions to grant loans to pay for this rainforest destruction were made with no review from either environmental experts or the local people who would be directly affected. Beginning in 1987, however, the World Bank began a program of reforms, including mandatory review of proposals by environmental experts—both in industrialized nations and where the project will take place—and a requirement to fund more environmentally unharmful development projects. Although conservationists have criticized the bank for not implementing these reforms fast enough, the changes nevertheless represent a long-overdue step in the right direction.

In 1990 the World Bank went one step further. In addition to trying to avoid highly destructive rainforest projects, the organization began a new program, in collaboration with the United Nations, that makes up to $400 million a year available for projects that help protect the forests. Such projects would include schemes to harvest nonwood forest products sustainably and debt-for-nature swaps to provide money for rainforest reserves and other conservation efforts.

GETTING TO THE ROOTS OF FOREST LOSS

When it comes to progress toward solving the root causes of deforestation, the news is much less encouraging. As discussed in chapter 5, the farmer, rancher, or logger who actually cuts down a rainforest often has no choice in the matter. Most tropical developing nations today are plagued by serious problems of overpopulation, unfair land distribution, and foreign debt. Poor farmers, for example, most likely have no land of their own to grow food and no money to buy any. They are thus forced to clear publicly owned forests—even in national parks if they can get away with it—or to invade them for products to sell in order to feed their families.

Obviously, curbing population growth and redistributing wealth and land would help relieve the pressure the landless poor put on tropical rainforests. But these goals are much easier stated than achieved, and, in most developing nations, progress toward such reforms is slow to nonexistent. Industrialized nations such as the United States and Canada could help. One way would be to provide more funding for family planning, education, and anti-poverty programs. Industrialized countries that grant or lend money to developing countries could also pressure those nations to redistribute land by making such action a condition of the grant or loan.

Perhaps the most important step the industrialized world could take to help tropical nations slow deforestation is to provide these countries some relief on their huge foreign debts—to stop, as tropical ecologist Peter Raven of the Missouri Botanical Garden puts it, "a blood transfusion from the sick to the healthy." Recently, the United States took a few steps in this direction by instituting the Brady Plan, an offer of new financing for developing countries that have large foreign debts. Costa Rica, one of the first nations to participate in the plan, should be able to save $150 million a year. Even so, Costa Rica, which owes a total of $1.8 billion, and other developing nations need much more help paying off their debts. These debts are not only encouraging countries to mine their rainforests for quick cash, they are also taking money away from conservation programs and from programs to raise the living standards of the poor.

INTERNATIONAL EFFORTS

As the examples given in this chapter make clear, there is a role for everyone when it comes to protecting the world's remaining rainforests. By necessity, the governments of tropical nations must be involved in some of the most critical actions: setting aside forest parks and reserves, regulating commercial logging, and redistributing land so that landless farmers are not forced to invade the rainforests, for example. But there is plenty of room for private efforts, too, as projects such as iguana ranching, the ecologically sound farming methods of Mexico's Maya Indians, and the boost to sustainable forest management provided by Ben & Jerry's demonstrate.

Given the economic interdependence of nations today, some of the most important steps needed to stop deforestation will have to be taken by governments working together. In recent years several encouraging precedents have been set. In 1985, for example, the governments of several nations—both tropical and temperate—launched a massive global action plan to establish protected areas in tropical nations, promote better forest management, and take other rainforest-conservation measures. Sponsored by the World Bank, the United Nations, and the World Resources Institute, the Tropical Forest Action Plan by 1990 had the participation of 70 countries and had raised several million dollars for rainforest conservation worldwide. Another unprecedented international effort, the International Tropical Timber Organization, includes the governments of nations that produce as well as consume tropical timber. It is the only commodity-oriented organization in the world with conservation as one of its major goals.

HOW CAN ONE PERSON HELP?

Because the problem of tropical deforestation is so enormous and its causes are so many and complex, the solutions can seem far beyond the reach of the average person—particularly those who live far from the tropics in the industrialized world. But in fact there is a great deal that every individual in every country can do to help. The citizens of industrialized nations, which control so much of the world's finances and natural resources, have a particular role to play. No action, no matter how small, is insignificant because, taken together, they have the potential to solve one of the world's biggest environmental problems. Below are a few suggestions.

- Find out more. First of all, learn all you can about rainforests and deforestation. Only the best-informed citizens can convince others that this problem is serious. Learn more about the tropical nations that house rainforests, including their difficult social and economic problems. (The books listed on pages 124–5 are a good place to start.) Check current newspapers and magazines for the most recent developments on deforestation.
- Spread the word. Let your family, neighbors, and friends know of your concern for tropical rainforests. Organize lectures, movies, slide shows, poster exhibits, and other activities in your school. Do a term paper or class project. Encourage teachers to make rainforests and deforestation a part of their biology curriculum.
- Contact public officials. Let your elected representatives know that you are concerned about tropical deforestation. Ask them what they are doing to help solve the problem. Letters to the heads of committees that sponsor legislation

The World Bank and similar organizations are under increasing pressure to stop funding development projects that damage rainforests and other threatened habitats.

affecting rainforests can also help; find out which new laws are being considered, and let committee members know your position on these proposals.

∘ Join conservation organizations. Hundreds of local, national, and international groups are working to save tropical rainforests. Contact some of these organizations (see list of addresses on pages 122–3) to find out more about what they do.

∘ Be a careful consumer. Ask retailers if the furniture and other tropical timber products they sell have come from plantations or carefully managed natural forests. If not— or if retailers do not know where their merchandise came from—do not buy their products and let them know why. Find out about the Seal of Approval that the organization Friends of the Earth awards to companies that obtain tropical wood products from sustainable sources; tell retailers how they can participate in the program. If you buy tropical plants or pets, buy only those that have been raised in captivity. Again, if retailers do not know where an exotic bird or other animal came from, do not buy it and let the store owner know of your concerns.

PERSONAL RESPONSIBILITY

Each of these actions, if taken by thousands of individuals, would make a tremendous contribution. But perhaps even more important than actions aimed specifically at saving rainforests is the way each person lives his or her own life. For poor, tropical nations, protecting rainforests will mean some significant sacrifices—such as giving up much-needed income from logging or from converting forests to plantations or cattle ranches. How can these struggling nations be expected to make such sacrifices if the citizens of rich nations are not willing to make sacrifices as well?

One of the arguments tropical nations hear most often to convince them not to cut down rainforests is that destruction of those forests releases large amounts of carbon dioxide, which enhances the greenhouse effect that scientists believe is causing global temperatures to rise. The effects of global warming are expected to be more severe in temperate than in tropical zones. Yet at the same time that industrialized nations ask tropical nations to forgo economic development in order to save rainforests, these rich nations have made little progress toward reducing their own carbon dioxide emissions. The United States, for instance, uses more energy and releases more carbon dioxide per person than any other country in the world.

Although correcting this inequity will certainly require strong measures from national governments—cutting power plant emissions, investing more in public transportation, and requiring auto makers to build more fuel-efficient cars, for example—citizens of the industrialized world can also do their part. If each individual were willing to drive less, turn thermostats down in winter and up in summer, and recycle paper and other trash, the collective impact would be significant—and would give tropical developing nations a sign that everyone is willing to make a few sacrifices of their own.

APPENDIX: FOR MORE INFORMATION

Environmental Organizations

Conservation International
1015 18th Street NW, Suite 1000
Washington, DC 20036
(202) 429-5660

Cultural Survival
11 Divinity Avenue
Cambridge, MA 02138
(617) 495-2562

Earthwatch
P.O. Box 403
Watertown, MA 02272
(617) 926-8200

Friends of the Earth
218 D Street SE
Washington, DC 20003
(202) 544-2600

The Nature Conservancy
1815 North Lynn Street
Arlington, VA 22209
(703) 841-5300

Rainforest Action Network
301 Broadway, Suite A
San Francisco, CA 94133
(415) 398-4404

Rainforest Alliance
270 Lafayette Street, Suite 512
New York, NY 10012
(212) 941-1900

Smithsonian Institution
National Museum of Natural
  History
Washington, DC 20560
(202) 357-1300

United Nations Environment
  Program
1889 F Street NW
Washington, DC 20006
(202) 289-8456

World Resources Institute
1709 New York Avenue NW,
  7th Floor
Washington, DC 20006
(202) 638-6300

Worldwatch Institute
1776 Massachusetts Avenue NW
Washington, DC 20036
(202) 452-1999

World Wildlife Fund/
  Conservation Foundation
1250 24th Street NW
Washington, DC 20037
(202) 293-4800

U.S. Government Agencies

Environmental Protection Agency
401 M Street SW
Washington, DC 20460
(202) 382-2090

U.S. International Development
  Cooperation Agency
320 21st Street NW
Washington, DC 20523

FURTHER READING

American Forestry Association. *American Forests*. Special issue on tropical deforestation (November/December 1988).

Caufield, Catherine. *In the Rainforest*. Chicago: University of Chicago Press, 1986.

Denslow, Julie Sloan, and Christine Padoch, eds. *People of the Tropical Rainforest*. Berkeley and Los Angeles: University of California Press (in association with the Smithsonian Institution Traveling Exhibition Service, Washington, DC), 1988.

Forsyth, Adrian, and Ken Miyata. *Tropical Nature: Life and Death in the Rain Forests of Central and South America*. New York: Scribners, 1984.

Gradwohl, Judith, and Russell Greenberg. *Saving the Tropical Forests*. London: Earthscan, 1988.

Head, Suzanne, and Robert Heinzman, eds. *Lessons of the Rainforest*. San Francisco: Sierra Club Books, 1990.

Hecht, Susanna, and Alexander Cockburn. *The Fate of the Forest: Developers, Destroyers, and Defenders of the Amazon*. London: Verso, 1989.

Jacobs, Marius. *The Tropical Rain Forest: A First Encounter*. Berlin: Springer-Verlag, 1988.

Miller, Kenton, and Laura Tangley. *Trees of Life: Saving Tropical Forests and Their Biological Wealth (A World Resources Institute Guide to the Environment)*. Boston: Beacon Press, 1991.

Mitchell, Andrew, W. *The Enchanted Canopy.* New York: Macmillan, 1986.

Myers, Norman. *The Primary Source: Tropical Forests and Our Future.* New York: Norton, 1984.

————. "Tropical Forests and their Species: Going, Going . . . ?" In *Biodiversity,* edited by E. O. Wilson. Washington, DC: National Academy Press, 1988.

National Geographic Society. *The Emerald Realm: Earth's Precious Rain Forests.* Washington, DC: National Geographic Society, 1990.

Perry, Donald. *Life Above the Jungle Floor.* New York: Simon & Schuster, 1986.

Postel, Sandra, and Lori Heise. *Reforesting the Earth* (Worldwatch Paper 83). Washington, DC: Worldwatch Institute, 1988.

Raven, Peter. "The Cause and Impact of Deforestation." In *Earth '88: Changing Geographic Perspectives.* Washington, DC: National Geographic Society, 1988.

————. "Our Diminishing Tropical Forests." In *Biodiversity,* edited by E. O. Wilson. Washington, DC: National Academy Press, 1988.

Wilson, E. O. "The Current State of Biological Diversity." In *Biodiversity,* edited by E. O. Wilson. Washington, DC: National Academy Press, 1988.

GLOSSARY

agroforestry   Agricultural system in which farmers plant trees among crops to help restore nutrients to the soil, control erosion and water flow, and provide shade for those crops.

biological diversity   The genetic variety of living species; the more species there are, the greater the degree of biological diversity; also known as biodiversity.

biosphere reserve   A type of protected area, first designed by United Nations scientists, that includes rather than excludes people. A typical reserve features several zones ranging from a strictly protected core zone to a transition zone, where communities of people live and use the reserve's natural resources.

debt-for-nature swap   A financial arrangement in which part of a developing country's foreign debt is bought at a discount by an outside party, such as an environmental organization. The debt is then remitted if the government undertakes activities to protect its environment.

deciduous forest   Forest in which trees lose all their leaves for several months, in response to seasonal climate changes.

ecosystem   An interdependent community of organisms living in a particular habitat, as well as the physical and chemical interactions within that community.

epiphyte   A plant that grows on another plant, using the host for support but not taking away any of its food or harming it in any other way.

evergreen forest   Forest in which trees maintain some of their leaves or needles throughout the year.

evolution   The process by which species adapt over time to changes in their environment. Physical and behavioral variations may occur in the offspring of organisms that make them better- or worse-suited to their environment—and thus more or less likely to survive and pass these new traits on to offspring of their own.

extractive reserve   A type of forest reserve that has been set aside for local people to harvest products such as rubber, fruit, and nuts that require the preservation rather than the destruction of rainforests.

germ plasm   Genetic material that can be passed on from one generation of plant or animal to another.

greenhouse effect   The trapping of infrared radiation in the earth's atmosphere by gases, such as carbon dioxide and methane, that results in higher atmospheric temperatures.

herbivore   An animal that feeds on plants.

indigenous   Originating or living naturally in a particular region or environment; native.

island biogeography   A theory that predicts the number of species that an island—or an isolated habitat that becomes like an island—can support based on how large the island or area is, how far it is from a mainland, and how long it has been isolated; the smaller, farther apart, and longer isolated an island or habitat is, the fewer species it can support.

monoculture   Agricultural fields that contain just one kind of crop. Typical of most large farms in industrialized nations today, mono-cultures require expensive fertilizers and pesticides because they drain the soil of nutrients and attract hordes of pests specialized to feed on just one kind of plant.

mycorrhizae   The feeding structures of fungi, which are attached to the roots of rainforest trees and to organic matter such as twigs, leaves, and animal and insect parts decaying on the ground; responsible for the efficient transfer of nutrients from dead to living material in the forest.

neotropics   The New World tropics of Central and South America and the Caribbean, as opposed to the Old World tropics of Africa, Asia, and Australia.

oxisol   A type of soil, commonly found in rainforests, that is poor in nutrients as a result of the continual leaching out of those nutrients by tropical rainfall.

parasite   Organisms that obtain their food by stealing nutrients from other organisms, harming or killing their hosts in the process.

photosynthesis   The process by which plants form simple carbohydrates from carbon dioxide, water, and nutrients, using sunlight as energy.

pollinators   Animals that carry pollen—the fertilizing element of flowering plants—from one plant to another, thereby enabling the plants to reproduce.

polyculture   An agricultural field in which many different crops are planted together, providing one another with benefits such as nutrients and natural pesticides; far more sustainable and ecologically sound than **monocultures**.

predators   Animals—as well as some plants—that feed on other animals.

primary forest   A forest that has not been previously cut down and regenerated, as opposed to a secondary forest, in which the original vegetation has been removed.

recombinant DNA technology   A process in which researchers move the basic units of heredity—DNA, packaged in a plant's or animal's genes—from one organism or species to another in order to create new traits to be passed on to future generations.

sustainable farms   Farms that continue producing food indefinitely without degrading the natural resources upon which they depend.

C o n v e r s i o n   T a b l e

(From U.S./English system units to metric system units)

Length

1 inch = 2.54 centimeters
1 foot = 0.305 meters
1 yard = 0.91 meters
1 statute mile = 1.6 kilometers (km.)

Area

1 square yard = 0.84 square meters
1 acre = 0.405 hectares
1 square mile = 2.59 square km.

Liquid Measure

1 fluid ounce = 0.03 liters
1 pint (U.S.) = 0.47 liters
1 quart (U.S.) = 0.95 liters
1 gallon (U.S.) = 3.78 liters

Weight and Mass

1 ounce = 28.35 grams
1 pound = 0.45 kilograms
1 ton = 0.91 metric tons

Temperature

1 degree Fahrenheit = 0.56 degrees Celsius or centigrade, but to convert from actual Fahrenheit scale measurements to Celsius, subtract 32 from the Fahrenheit reading, multiply the result by 5, and then divide by 9. For example, to convert 212° F to Celsius:

$$212 - 32 = 180 \times 5 = 900 \div 9 = 100° \text{ C}$$

INDEX

Africa, 24, 68, 87, 93, 100
African blackwood, 53
Agouti, 28
Agroforestry, 59
Amazon Basin, 39, 68, 84
Amazonia, 39, 52, 97, 100
Ambuklao Dam, 95
Animal life
    adaption to environment,
      41–42
    defense against predators,
      44–45
    extinction, 15, 99–101
    food, 41
    types, 28, 31–32, 35–36
Antbird, 48
Anteater, 31
Ants, 13, 28–29. *See specific*
    types
Arboreal life, 35
Army ant, 48–49
Ashton, Peter, 13
Asia, 68, 87, 93, 96, 100
Australia, 24, 82
Aztec ants, 44

Balbina Dam, 84
Bali, 85
Banana, 52
Bates, Henry Walter, 45
Batesian mimicry, 45
Bat flower, 46
Beetle, 37

Ben & Jerry's Homemade Ice
    Cream, Inc., 114
Biomass, 27
Biosphere reserve, 106
Bird of paradise, 35, 45–46
Birds
    diversity of species, 39
    mating rituals, 45–46
Black pepper, 52
Body Shop, The, 114
Bolivia, 108
Borneo, 85, 100, 112
Bower bird, 46
Brady Plan, 117
Brazil, 68, 83, 84–85, 88–89, 97,
    98, 100, 114
Bromeliad, 34–35
Burma, 53
Bushmaster, 28
Butterfly, 39
Butterfly flower, 46

Cacao, 59, 82
Cachi Dam, 95
California redwood tree, 26
Camouflage, 44–45
Canopy layer, 25, 33–36
Canopy tree, 42
Capuchin, 35
Capybara, 28
Carbon, 64
Carbon dioxide, 64–65, 121
Carrion fly, 47

Cash crop, 89
Cattle ranching, 81–83
    alternative methods, 110–11
Cecropia tree, 44
Central America, 24, 82, 93
Chameleon, 31, 42
Chiapas, Mexico, 59
Childhood leukemia, 56
Chlorofluorocarbons, 64
Chondrodendron tomentosum, 55
Cinchona tree, 55, 57
Cinnamon, 52
Clay, Jason, 114
Clothing, 55
Cloves, 52
Coatis, 31
Cocoa, 52
Coconut oil, 54
Coffee, 52, 82
Colombia, 25, 39, 100
Commercial logging, 69–79
    ban on, 94
    environmentally safer
        methods, 111–14
Conservation International, 108
Corn, 51, 52
Costa Rica, 30, 68, 107, 108, 110,
    117
Crabwood, 53
Cuaca Valley, Colombia, 95
Cuckoos, 48
Cultural Survival, 98

Darwin, Charles, 25–26, 40
Debt-for-nature swap, 108
Deciduous tropical forest, 24
Deforestation
    consequences, 91–101
    direct causes, 68–85

indirect causes, 86–89
    rate, 41, 67–68
Desert, 25
Drugs, 55–56, 57–58

Ebony, 53
Ecotourism, 107
Ecuador, 100, 108
Efe pygmies, 60
Emergent layer, 25
Emergents, 33
Epiphytic plants, 34, 42
Equator, 13, 23, 24
Erwin, Terry, 37
Ethiopia, 52
European colonists, 17
Evolution, 40–41
Extractive reserves, 114
Eyelash viper, 31

Farming
    environmentally safer
        methods, 109–110
    and indigenous groups,
        58–61, 79–80
    subsistence farming,
        79-80
    sustainable farming,
        58-59
Fer-de-lance, 28
Fig tree, 47
Fig wasp, 47
Fish, 42
Flooding, 93–94
Foreign debt, 70, 88–89, 108,117
Forest floor layer, 25–30
Fossil fuel, 65
Friends of the Earth, 120
Fuelwood, 79, 92–93

Gecko, 31
Germ plasm, 51
Ghana, 92
Gibbon, 35
Gillis, Malcolm, 69
Gold miners, 98
Grande Carajás mining project, 84
Grasslands, 25
Great Mormon caterpillar, 45
Greenhouse effect, 64–65
Guarea, 53

Hartshorn, Gary, 30
Hepatitis, 98
Herbivore, 43
Hevea brasiliensis tree, 54
Himalayas, 100
Hodgkin's disease, 56
Hornbill, 35, 46
Howling monkey, 35
Hummingbird, 31, 41
Hummingbird flowers, 46
Hydroelectirc dam, 83, 95, 115
Hydrologic cycle, 61–64

Ice age, 40
Iguana ranching, 111
India, 53
Indonesia, 13, 53, 69, 85, 93
Industrial development, 83–85
    environmentally safer
        methods, 115–16
Influenza, 97, 98
Insects, 27–28, 31, 37
    defense against predators,
        44–45
    social insects, 28–30
Inter-American Development
    Bank, 115

International Tropical Timber
    Organization, 118
Ireland, 53
Iron ore, 84
Island biogeography theory, 100
Ituri Forest, Zaire, 60
Ivory Coast, 68

Jacamar, 35
Jaguar, 31, 41
Jangala, 26
Japan, 53, 69
Java, 85, 95, 110

Katydid, 44
Kayapo, 59
Khaya, 52–53

Lacandon Maya Indians, 59, 110
Latin America, 68, 82, 87
Leaching, 27
Leaf-cutter ant, 28, 41
Lemur, 31
Leopard, 31
Lese, 60
Lessons of the Rainforest (Clay), 97
Lianas, 33–34, 42
Litter decomposition, 26–27
Lorikeet, 35
Loris, 31
Lua, 60–61

MacArthur, Robert, 100
Macaw, 35
Madagascar, 100
Mahogany, 52–53
Malaria, 57, 98
Malaysia, 69, 70, 93, 100
Malaysian praying mantis, 44
Manakin, 45

Mandibles, 28
Mangla Dam, 95
Mango, 52
Manure, 93
Marcos, Ferdinand, 94
Mars, 64
Mato Grosso (Brazil), 85
Measles, 97
Mendes, Chico, 114
Methane, 64
Mexico, 51, 93
Microclimate, 25
Milpas, 110
Mixed-species flocks, 42
Monarch butterfly, 45
Monkey, 35–36
Monoculture, 109
Moth, 44
Motmots, 48
Mycorrhizae, 27
Myers, Norman, 62, 64, 69, 82,
    100, 101, 111

National Cancer Institute, 55
Natural selection, 40
Nature Conservancy, The, 108
Neotropics, 36
Netherlands, The, 53
New Caledonia, 100
New Guinea, 57, 85
New Zealand, 24, 82
Nigeria, 68, 92
Nitrogen-fixing plants, 110
Nitrous oxide, 64
Nutmeg, 52

Ocelot, 31
Orange, 52
Orangutan, 35
Orchid, 34, 41

Origin of Species, The (Darwin),
    40
Oropendola, 35
Ouabain, 55
Overpopulation, 19, 86–87
Oxisols, 27
Ozone, 64

Paca, 28
Pakistan, 95
Palm oil, 54, 82
Panama, 39, 110
Panama Canal, 95
Papaya, 52
"Paper parks," 106
Parasite, 34
Parrot, 35, 41
Passion flower, 44
Peccary, 28
Pekarangan, 110
Peru, 13, 37, 39, 51, 113
Philippines, 69, 70, 93–94, 95,
    100, 108
Phosphorous, 27
Photosynthesis, 33
Pioneer tree species, 30, 42
Plant life
    defense against predators,
    43–44
    diversity of species, 39
    and drugs, 55–56
    food source, 42
    germination, 47
    pollination, 46–47
    types, 33–35
Poison dart frog, 45, 46
Pollinators, 46
Polyculture, 110
Potassium, 27
Potato, 51

Potoo, 35
Prehensile tail, 36
Primary rainforest, 109
Primary Source, The (Myers), 62

Quetzal, 35
Quinine, 55, 57

Rafflesia arnoldi, 46–47
Raven, Peter, 117
Recombinant DNA, 56–57
Reid, Walter, 100
Rice, 51, 93
Rondônia (Brazil), 85
Rosewood, 53
Rosy periwinkle, 55
Rubber, 54–55, 59

Sapele, 53
Secondary compounds, 43–44, 55
Secondary rainforest, 109
Sedimentation, 95–96
Shifting cultivation, 80
Slash-and-burn agriculture. *See*
    Shifting cultivation
Sloth, 35, 36, 39
Smithsonian Tropical Research
    Institute, 110–11
Snakes, 28
Soil erosion, 62, 80, 95
South America, 24, 96, 100
Southeast Asia, 24, 51, 82
    and logging, 69–79
Southern corn leaf blight, 51–52
Spider monkey, 35
Strangler fig, 43
Strophanthus gratus, 55
Sugarcane, 82
Sumatra, 85
Sunbird, 31

Tarantula, 28
Teak, 52–53
Termite, 28
Thailand, 53, 60, 94
Torrid Zone, 23
Toucan, 35, 41
Trade winds, 24
Transpiration, 63
Tree boa, 31
Tree fall gap, 30–31
Tree frog, 31
Tree kangaroo, 31
Trees, 13, 26, 30, 39
Trogon, 35
Tropical dry forest. *See* Deciduous
    tropical forest
Tropical Forest Action Plan, 118
Tropical hardwood
    exportation, 69, 92
    types, 52–54
Tropical rainforest
    annual rainfall, 25
    and biotechnology, 56–57
    climate, 25
    diversity of species, 39–40
    indigenous groups, 57–61,
      79–80, 96–99
    layers, 25–37
    location, 23–25
    nonwood products, 54–57
    preservation solutions,
      105–121
    species interdependence,
      47–49
    and worldwide climate
      regulation, 64–65
    and worldwide water supply,
      61–64
Tropic of Cancer, 23
Tropic of Capricorn, 23

Tuberculosis, 97, 98
Tubocurarine, 55

Uatumá River, 84
Understory layer, 25, 30–32
United Nations, 118
United Nations Educational,
    Scientific, and Cultural
    Organization (UNESCO), 106
United Nations Food and
    Agriculture Organization
    (FAO), 67, 79
United States
    beef consumption, 82
    hardwood consumption,
    53–54, 69
    primary forests, 14
    and rainforest protection,
    116–117
Utile, 53

Veneers, 52

Venezuela, 98
Venus, 64
Viceroy butterfly, 45
Vine snake, 31

Water vapor, 64
Whooping cough, 97
Wilson, E. O., 13, 100
Winged bean, 57
Woodcreeper, 48
Woolly monkey, 35
World Bank, 83, 84, 85, 88, 115,
    118
World Resources Institute,
    118
World Resources 1990–91,
    67
World Wildlife Fund, 108

Yanomami, 98

Zaire, 60

PICTURE   CREDITS

AP/Wide World Photos: pp. 81, 96; Dave Augeri/© Greenpeace: pp. 70, 75, 86; Courtesy Ben & Jerry's: p. 114; Rob Bierregaard: pp. 18, 36, 63; © James L. Castner: pp. 12, 22, 26, 29, 31, 42, 45, 49, 50, 55, 60, 66, 77 (bottom), 78 (bottom), 88, 90, 108; Courtesy Department of Library Services, American Museum of Natural History: p. 21 (neg. # 119317); © Buddy Mays/TRAVEL STOCK: pp. 38, 58, 74 (bottom); Plowden/© Greenpeace: p. 99; Courtesy Rainforest Action Network: pp. 72, 73, 94, 119; Reuters/Bettmann Archive: p. 103; Gary Tong: pp. 14–15; © Norbert Wu, 1991: pp. 32, 43, 71, 72–73; 74 (top), 76 (top and bottom), 77 (top), 78 (top), 104, 113

ABOUT THE AUTHOR

LAURA TANGLEY is a science writer with a long-standing interest in the conservation of forests and other ecosystems, particularly in the tropics. Over the past 10 years, she has written many articles on these subjects for publications such as *Science News, BioScience, Issues in Science and Technology*, and *Earthwatch* and currently works as a freelance writer and staff member at Conservation International in Washington, D.C. With Kenton Miller of the World Resources Institute, Tangley coauthored a book on tropical forests, *Trees of Life: Saving Tropical Forests and Their Biological Wealth,* published in 1991.

ABOUT THE EDITOR

RUSSELL E. TRAIN, currently chairman of the board of directors of the World Wildlife Fund and The Conservation Foundation, has had a long and distinguished career of government service under three presidents. In 1957 President Eisenhower appointed him a judge of the United States Tax Court. He served Lyndon Johnson on the National Water Commission. Under Richard Nixon he became under secretary of the Interior and, in 1970, first chairman of the Council on Environmental Quality. From 1973 to 1977 he served as administrator of the Environmental Protection Agency. Train is also a trustee or director of the African Wildlife Foundation; the Alliance to Save Energy; the American Conservation Association; Citizens for Ocean Law; Clean Sites, Inc.; the Elizabeth Haub Foundation; the King Mahendra Trust for Nature Conservation (Nepal); Resources for the Future; the Rockefeller Brothers Fund; the Scientists' Institute for Public Information; the World Resources Institute; and Union Carbide and Applied Energy Services, Inc. Train is a graduate of Princeton and Columbia Universities, a veteran of World War II, and currently resides in the District of Columbia.